an
ANTHOLOGY
of
POEMS
and
ARTICLES

by
LAWRENCE L. BAND

Camp Skymark
an anthology of poems and articles

Copyright ©2016 Lawrence L. Band.

All rights reserved, including the right to reproduce this book or portions thereof in any form.

ISBN: 978-0-9952345-1-2

Camp Skymark is a work of fiction. Certain incidents described in this book are based on actual recent and historical events, but other than well-known public figures referred to by name, all the characters are products of the author's imagination. Any resemblance to anyone in real life is unintentional and purely coincidence. No part of this book may be reproduced, or stored in a retrieval system, or transmitted in any form or by any means, electronic, mechanical, photocopied, recorded, or otherwise, without express written permission of the author.

This book is typeset in Arial, Times New Roman and Nyx.

Editing, Interior Design and Layout by: Russell Phillips,
The Creative Source
(www.scourcedesign.com)

Cover Design by: Russell Phillips

Acknowledgements

I have had a great deal of help and encouragement from several sources in developing and bringing this book to fruition. Those most involved were Dr. Phil Fleishman, Sol Jakubowicz, Myron Sidenberg, Eleanor Kunigis (Moidel), my amazing wife, Sheila and my editor, Russell Phillips.

Dr. Phil Fleishman is a retired plastic surgeon, and an accomplished author. He has written two excellent novels and has freely and generously given me useful suggestions and advice. He has repeatedly urged me to put together an anthology of some of my poems and then publish it. I finally gave in to him because, we have been best friends for over 60 years, and if he had the tenacity not to give up on that friendship, he would never give up on urging me to write this book. I am deeply indebted to him for his kind support.

Sol and Myron are friends who played the good cop/bad cop critics. I won't tell who the bad cop was, but together their critical analysis was a major help to me as they provided, third party insights and opinions resulting in many improvements to the book.

Eleanor (Ellie) locked up the meaning, spelling and translation of the several Yiddish words and phrases used herein. She is a keen educator in, and teacher of, the Yiddish language and Jewish culture. Her excellent work resulted in many enhancements of the book's content.

My wife, Sheila, is a most amazing woman mother and wife. She has helped me in every way possible to get this book published. She appears as the subject in several of the poems. I did that in recognition of her important place in my life and to underscore the wonderful person she is. I suspect she may have expended the great deal of energy she did, to ensure that there would be nothing in the style or format of the book that detracted from its relevant content.

Russell Phillips is a Floridian and editor/designer whose services I am happy I engaged on the advice of a friend. Russell is an intelligent, skillful artist and publisher. He is an honest and seasoned professional in whom I have much confidence and with whom I find it a pleasure to work.

To my editor, Russell
Full of hustle and bustle
Or is it hassle and tussle
No matter, and whatever,
He has a mind exceptionally adept and clever.
And he's skilled and adroit enough to endeavour
To bring amateur original works that are artsy-fartsy
Down-to- earth, in a way that's realistically smartsy
To transform the same into wording beautifully written and clear
And to fine tune them into literature
Worthy of a modern day Shakespeare.

 I express my heartfelt appreciation to all of you for your help.
Thank you so very much!

To:

My wife, Sheila;
My daughter Michelle and her partner, Malcolm;
My son Michael and daughter-in-law, Holly;
My son David;
My grandchildren, Joshua, Avery, Sam, Olivia, Kevin and Morgan;
My sister, Geitel and her partner, Joe.

A day without laughter is a day wasted.

— Charley Chaplin

Introduction:

On turning 75, my children presented me with a license plate as a birthday gift. On it was inscribed, "Where am I?" After that, several kindly people at various different times and places, on seeing the plate on my car, would approach me to let me know where I was. Their concern always made me feel good, if not enlightened.

In any event, I never thought that the answer to the question as to where I was at any given point was nearly as important as the answer to the question, who am I? That is difficult to answer. So much depends on the perceptions you create arising from what you say and do, what you have said and done, the consistency, if any, in that conduct, and the personal make-up of the perceiver.

There is no doubt that part of who I am is embraced in my history, including that I am a 78 year old retired lawyer and, a former judicial officer, sitting as a Member of The Immigration and Refugee Board of Canada. I am a Canadian citizen who loves Canada dearly. As well, I am a family man, married blissfully to the same woman for 56 years, a father of three adult children and grandfather of six grandchildren. In short I am a very lucky man.

However, I am more than just a factual history of my being. I have used my poems partially to disclose that extra me. I have opened some of my thoughts about myself and of others, as well as the hodgepodge of topics about which I chose to write.

You are not likely to find any reason as to the choice of subjects of the poems or as to their order of appearance, although I do hope that you will find some rhyme in them. To put the poems in logical order or to group them under some specific categories would be to bespeak of an order that is absent in my life.

The title, Camp Skymark refers to the condominium that my wife and I moved into about 11 years ago. We've made many good friends at Skymark. It is such a fun place to live in that it's more akin to a kid's recreational camp than an adult condominium. It is a place full of wonderful and long-suffering friends who have put up with my puns, my love of laughter and of making others laugh, as well as my obsessive love of the hot dog.

POEMS AND ARTICLES

-1-

I wrote this poem to acknowledge the efforts of many of my friends who took the time to reply to my e-mails that contained poems with their own unique poetry. Thank you!

Poetry Is Fun. Isn't It?

Poetry is fun. Isn't it?
As it is enjoyed, I submit,
By wise men and idiots,
By geniuses and half-wits.

It's a multi-purpose disciplined craft
And I employ its many varied uses
Not to subject the readers to snide abuses,
But in fun, as a means to drive them daft.

Poetry is fun. Isn't it?
As it is enjoyed, I submit,
By wise men and idiots,
By geniuses and half-wits.

Today I penned my three hundredth plus rhyme.
Not poetry of the Shakespearean sonnets or time.
Nor designed for the artistically and seriously self-indulgent literati.
No, mine are pop-verses, of common topics that are light and breezy.

Poetry is fun. Isn't it?
As it is enjoyed, I submit,
By wise men and idiots,
By geniuses and half-wits.

Now lucky me, I'm getting replies,
In rhyme from all of you hip guys.
To my poems sent via your e-mail,
Leaving for me and for my detail,
To determine into what category you accurately fit.
Is it the wise man or idiot? The genius or the half-wit?

-2-

   Many litigants do not understand what the difference is between justice and the law. Most litigants believe that if they won their lawsuits they have received justice. On the other hand if their lawyers lost the lawsuits it was because their lawyers and the law jointly and severally are arses.

Neither Justice Nor Law

To a lawyer it is one thing to freely act and opine
And very different to opine and act for free.
The former is considered a professional propensity
And the latter is rejected as un-billable time.

In the Courts where serious issues are tried,
It is the law and not justice that is applied.
In addition, if in Court, justice overcomes injustice in such fight,
It is more a result of coincidence than a cause-and-effect vindication of right.

Additionally, exorbitant lawyers' and other related Court fees,
Coupled with lengthy delays in resolving laws' complexities,
Shamefully render our legal system a dysfunctional mess,
Effectively depriving citizens of meaningful Court access.

And litigants dispossessed of trial in a traditional Court
May out of despair and frustration to violence resort
And engage in trial by battle on the street
Subjecting our society to its greatest defeat.

-3-

If you love the beauty and the cyclic nature of Nature, Canada is the place to be.

Inward, Outward and Downward Bound

There is nothing in nature more beautiful than seeing,
The flapping wings of our Canadian honkers beating.

In V-shaped formations as northward and homeward bound, they wing
Singing and honking as they portend the enchanting sounds of Spring.

Yet, in Autumn, there is little in Nature that will more displease,
Than seeing beautifully coloured leafs dropping from their trees.

Or than the departure of our lovely Canadian geese.
Fleeing Canada in a flight-pattern of contrived Vees.

And Man has no magical powers to alter or stem this ebb and flow,
As Nature ordains and instinct compels, the leafs and birds must go.

And so, obedient and true,
To their nature, they do.

As for Man, his ineffective instincts are not for him a moving force
Instead he relies on his reason and intuition as his guiding resource.

Thus as Man lacks the infallibility and blind certainty that animal instinct brings,

His failure to arrive at his life's destination is more than just one of those things.

-4-

It seems that my wife has embraced the finer aspects of the Chinese American cultures. She plays Mah Jongg and eats Chinese noodles and is addicted to both.

Languishing at Home Alone

Here I am languishing at home
Been married for 56 very happy years.
But now uncharacteristically alone,
And sadly shedding waterfall tears.

Inconsolable am I, as it is our anniversary
And my bride of more than half a century
Has flown the coop, has gone away
On this our most auspicious day.

To add insult to injury, and the obtuse to the obscene.
She's holding Court with dragons, red, white and green.
Playing with all those O's, bams and cracks
While munching on sweets and salty snacks.

Removing the N.E.W.S. directional tiles from her rack
Manipulating the lovely flower tiles by way of attack,
Whilst doing battle with her playmates, the jokers four.
And keeping in reserve for insurance needs, eight more.

Sober thought has led me to truly perceive
That I on this my spoiled anniversary eve
Have suffered a most demeaning wrong
Being a reject, in favour of Mah Jongg.

Even so, I wish you a happy anniversary, my lovely dear,
And although what you have done, may seem a little queer.
I'd consider you not to be a very terrible sinner,
If you'd come home as one really huge winner.

-5-

My friend asked what I would be like on my 100th birthday, and I responded:

The View From My 75th Birthday

By my 100th birthday what will be my condition?
I can't say for certain but I do have a premonition.

My buns will be saggy
My gait will be *draggy*.

My hearing fast fading
My muscles degrading

My thinning hair
No longer there

And my deliberate, measured, slowed, advance
Will make others feel I'm in a perpetual trance.

Your ears will get sore,
As I'll likely talk more.

But throughout all of the while
I'll forever wear a happy smile.

It's impossible that I will not.
As I appreciate what I've got.

A really great family, and many a good friend.
Much cause to give thanks and saying an *amen*.

-6-

   A friend, while in Shanghai, sent me photographs of the super-structures built into the fabric of that city. He asked me for relevant comments on the contents of those photos in the context of China's history.

China

A society that values and stresses
Its infrastructure over the masses.
People control
Over the soul.
Quickly arrives, and likewise passes.

While metamorphosing through its turbulent history,
Transiting intolerably onward from misery to misery.
Subdued and imprisoned throughout the ages,
In super-infrastructures of gold-rimmed cages.

Is there a difference between old and aging?

Not Old, Just Aging

Am I and have I become old?
As just recently, I've been told.

In addition, will I be an unwanted and an unread book,
Unceremoniously to be shelved in some corner nook?

Just left there, I trust,
To collect some dust.

No, that will not be me,
Nor remotely my destiny.

As I have always lived independently happy.
And at all times I've certainly been dust-free.

I've not gotten old, although I have aged.
Even so, my life remains fully engaged.

With a beautiful and enchanting wife,
Who enhances every moment of my life

And with great offspring, the next generation
Of this our fabulous and magnificent nation.

The joys of life I now experience remain undiminished,
Fully augmented by memories so vivid and cherished.

Moreover I can act on them as I have always wished,
Alive, and moving forward on those dreams yet unfinished

I have yet a myriad of things that remain undone,
With ample time to do them and still have fun.

So hopefully providence will extend and delay
My time for shelving to a much later day.

-8-

No one should worry about problems to which he can do nothing to change or to resolve.

What, Me Worry?

Worrying about the negative
Is not a positive way to live.
For sure, it's not for me,
So I'll not a worrier be.

Experience has made of me a wise sage
Knowing that the worst advancing age
Has done in any serious negative way to me
Is to make it more difficult to hear and to see.

I'll still laugh and refuse to cry,
That will be me without a lie.
With twinkles in my eyes,
With wrinkles I'll despise,
With smiles on my lips,
Contemplating my ever expanding hips.

In addition, as time goes by speedily,
I will be consuming most greedily
Amusement of every diverse kind,
Fed by an active and fertile mind.

Furthermore, let the groaners continue to groan.
I am too content with my life at this milestone.
So let the sceptics indulge in their scepticism.
Not me. I refuse to live in such a dark schism.

-9-

If you drive a Lamborghini sports car through a flood-prone valley, you are just as likely to be soaking wet as well as deep in debt.

The Hipster

He prides himself as an active speedster,
Sitting proud and tall behind his auto's wheel.
Decked in clothes giving him the look and feel
Of a daredevil, macho and stylish hipster.

He drives his convertible with roof down,
While presenting as a well-healed clown.
Wearing a gaudy pink and purple silken cravat,
A multi-coloured sculptured and checkered hat.

As he passes, he smiles and waves his odd beanie,
Revving the loud engine of his red-hot Lamborghini.
And as he does, you ask, what the devil was that?
Parading as a caricature of some cool cat.

When torrents of stormy rain,
Quickly and suddenly came.
He then slowed the car's speed,
Stopped to satisfy the urgent need
To bring down the roof swiftly without any hitch.

Instead it stalled in the rain in a deep-flooded ditch.

Inside the car, the water rose to his lap.
He hastily released his seat-belt strap
And, without much aplomb, abandoned ship,
Along with all appearances of his being hip.

All he wanted to do then was to get home
And immediately use a working land phone
To obtain advice and a firm assurance
That his loss was covered by his insurance.

-10-

A friend wanted to know if I was a lexophile, as I so much enjoyed puns and words, and if I was, could I do something about it?

The Lexophile

I thought about it for a while.
And then re-read with a smile
What you wrote.
And in response, wish to note.

Yes, certainly, I am an avid lexophile.
But that is better by a country mile,
In substantive essence and in pith,
Than being a boring wordsmith.

A lexophile, as facts have shown,
Cleverly expounds what is known
In a manner that's sharp and witty.
Whereas a wordsmith's pronouncements

Are absent meaningful linguistic enhancements.
And full of senseless and dull nitty-gritty.

So if you are complaining about my style,
I am, nonetheless happy to be a lexophile.
As I could have been much more vile...
Namely, both a wordsmith and lexophile.

-11-

Is there any flower more beautiful in its simplicity and more complex in its symbolic expressions than the rose?

The Rose

I am sitting here in the sun's brilliant light
Staring at an engaging and beautiful sight.

Swaying in the breeze, not far from the shadows,
Is a uniquely sculptured thorny blood red rose.

A strong perfumed aroma carries my way on a calm and gentle breeze,
As though being in place solely for me, and for all of my senses to please.

However, that is not so as it is too narrow a net to cast,
Considering the rose's place in Man's heart in the past.

A rose is the flowered symbol of conjugal love in magnificent bloom.
A whorled garland fit for a beautiful bride and her handsome groom.

Forever present to beautify and enhance Man's important events,
A unique flower of unparalleled beauty and absent all pretence.

Which provides a worthy reward for our noses,
When we take time to stop and smell the roses.

-12-

Our marriage began with an epiphany that triggered 56 years of a matrimonial harmony that blossomed into a waltz to which we are still dancing.

My One and Only

Fortunately, for me,
At age twenty-three,
I had an epiphany.
And fell in love with the woman of my destiny.

She mirrors the essence reflecting all of my dreams.
She is the justifying end for all of my means.
She is the sun and the moon that lights up my life.
She is my beautiful and long-suffering wife.

-13-

Be careful with your choice of words. For example, any medical operation that you may have had and which you describe as a simple one, might lead to someone thinking that you had brain surgery.

The Colonoscopy

Congratulations on your successful operation,

Ending your bouts of recurring frustration.
Which I am ecstatic and very pleased now to hear,
Has become epilogue, with little left for you to fear.

You have my total sympathies
For the multitude of miseries
Experienced in the process of preparation
For your dreaded colonoscopy operation.

I knew that, since you are so full of it,
You would for many hours have to sit,
Pushing, moaning and groaning whilst sadly all alone,
Working your iPhone whilst on your residential throne.

I learned since the long-awaited colonoscopy cutting day,
Your operation was performed in a most dangerous way,
In that it was undertaken so close to the locale of your brains,
That it was a miracle it cured your *fundamental orifice* strains.

While quite groggy, at the end of your operation procedure,
You informed me that you could've avoided this surgical cure,
As your rectal problems your doctor now definitively thinks
Were caused by consuming concentrated orange juice drinks.

So now, you drink strained and pulp-free orange juice only,
As their pulp was what triggered your pesky colonoscopy.
But I beg to say my dear friend, that just isn't realistically so.
You must've misunderstood what your doctor let you know.

As post-operatively, your head was in a foggy mist,
And you totally misunderstood your proctologist.
When he said that your problem was caused by a polyp
And not by an orange's pulp.

In any event, my dear good and kind friend,
And no matter how you may cut it in the end.

Let me now, sympathetically you console,
As alas, you no longer are a perfect A-hole.

-14-

Though each person is a composite of features and parts, and although each such feature and part, when considered individually is very important, it is nonetheless true, as the bible has expressed, that a woman's hair is her crowning glory.

Hair

Sheila you are beautiful whatever colour your hair is.
Whether auburn, streaked white or otherwise colour-toned.
You are, and will remain for all time, my enchanting princess,
And no hair colour change will cause you to be dethroned.

It matters little whether I like your new look.
What counts is that it pleases and makes you happy.
But in my humble opinion and for the book,
That colour makes you look quite fashionably snappy.

There is one thing that I must know,
And that is, after all is said and done.
Could you please opine,
In the fullness of time,
Whether it is really so,
That blondes do have more fun?

It has been so cold this winter that the dogs have been sticking to the fire hydrants and the scientists are using global warming to unglue them.

Global Warming?

For sure, Man's activity is causing our orb to warm.
What's going on in Boston, Miami and in our home,
Certainly proves that, without any question or any doubt,
Our raging North American winter has lost all of its clout.

Boston presently has almost six feet of heavy, white snow,
With more of it now falling and with no place for it to go.
And in the style of Bostonian anti-tax, revolutionary ingenuity,
They are disposing of it in the harbour as though it was iced tea.

If that's not proof enough that our warming is global,
Take notice and be concerned about Miami's cold wall
Of abnormally and ongoing low temperatures of brutal icy degrees,
Falling so low in Fahrenheit that it causes orange crops to freeze.

However, the strongest proof of the man-made warming of our orb
Is something that even the unscientific mind can most easily absorb.
It is Toronto's winter heat wave that causes our Torontonians to feel alive
As its winter temperatures with wind chill dips below minus thirty-five.

-16-

Canadians are lucky that cows can't fly.

Don't Pooh Pooh Our Canada Goose

Toronto at springtime is oh so unpleasantly loose,
As it hosts the graceful bowel-active Canada Goose.

Its droppings are smaller than that of elephants or mules,
But sadly appear all over as fowl smelling watery stools.

The goose has dark coloured feathers, very short legs and a curved throat,
An odd shaped beak through which is occasionally heard a honking note.

They're Canada's namesake and truly wonderful birds.
Until of course, you step into one of their liquid turds.

-17-

   If you worship a hot dog, are you an atheist? If you water-down that worship by adding a bun, do you simply become an agnostic? Moreover, if you add mustard and relish, do you become elevated to a gourmet?

The Hot Dog

I am a worshiper of the all beef wiener,
A doubting Thomas and non-believer.
I embrace my atheism with great relief,
And with a moral and ethical belief.

As every second Thursday, I anxiously nourish my soul's revival,

And attend at a small kiosk hot dog shrine to ensure my survival.
There to undergo an unholy, but tasteful dialogue,
With a diet coke and all beef, un-kosher hot dog.

That is wrapped in a non-wafer bun,
Which I will before I am fully done,
Faithfully, and truly embellish
With much mustard and relish,

And quickly down it knowing full well,
That, by not believing in heaven or hell,
If I am surreptitiously taken or removed from life's ebb and flow,
The worst I will suffer is being all dressed up—with no place to go.

-18-

I have always thought living was all about starting, becoming, doing, being and ending...and enjoying good meals in the meantime.

Has Been or Never Was?

Here next following is my latest buzz,
Activating my mind in a moment serene,
Concluding that it's better to be a has-been
Than a never-was.

What's the difference, you ask?
A has-been engages in and completes life's task,
And at the end of his time, here on this earth,
He leaves a legacy of some value and worth.

But a never-was, although physically and mentally present,
Rarely experiences Mankind's rhythmic rise and descent,

On any plane other than self-aggrandizement,
And rejects helping others as a needless impediment,
To the vision of his selfish and empty fulfillment.

So is it better to be the former than the latter?
The vicissitudes of life as seen through history
Are descriptive of Mankind's alternating joy and misery,
And as such, suggests that it really doesn't matter.

But I disagree, as to me, it does.
I cannot exist as a never-was.
It is in my genes to live fully and altruistically in my skin,
As I did in the past, but do now, as a retired happy has-been.

-19-

There is certainly pain in going on vacation and leaving friends behind, and then returning as they leave on vacation and you stay behind.

A Journey To The Sun

Adieu,
To you.

We leave on the morrow,
And, do so with sorrow.

It's getting unseasonably cold and *lateth*,
Soon it'll be January the twenty-*eighteth*,

When we will off to sunny Florida go,
And leave the cold and freezing snow.

I'm told the temperature there is seventy to seventy-five,
A hot sun, a cool wind and a very good time to be alive.

We'll grieve that here you'll not feel just quite the same,
But then, what are good friends for, if not to feel your pain.

So we wish for you all to have lots of fun too,
While were off getting our sun-browned hue.

We know that when our wonderful holidays are complete,
Selfishly, you'll start yours in the skin-burning Florida heat.

Leaving both of us here in Toronto with absolutely nothing to do.
More proof that there is not a single drop of loyalty in any of you.

-20-

This poem earned me three consecutive dinners of terrific chicken wings from my wife, and now I wonder what would happen if I wrote a poem extolling the great job she does making the beds.

Chicken Wings

What are all those many baked things?
My gosh! They're baked chicken wings.

Multiple wings? You may ask why?
Since chickens are unable to fly.

Indeed, all that they ever could do,
Was every day, lay an egg or two.

Cackle, peck or loudly crow,
And eventually then,

Whether rooster or hen
In the oven they'd go.

The value of their being is in the main,
A useful item in man's food chain.

Packaged into parts that suits man best.
Of chicken wings, drumsticks or breasts.

But to me here and now, I must say,
That I did, on this very tasteful day,

Dine on the best-baked chicken in all of the land
Made by my wife, the gourmet chef, Sheila Band!

-21-

Adam lost a rib when Eve was created. They ate of the forbidden fruit, the apple, at the urging of an evil serpent. Adam and Eve were ejected from the Garden of Eden, and they and their children suffered, as is chronicled in the history of Mankind. As for the evil serpent's punishment, it too was evicted from the Garden, and many of its progeny are found as worms or half worms, in partly eaten apples.

The Old Apple Tree Of Despair

No, the fruit of knowledge
Was not found at a college.
No, it hung in Eden on an old apple tree,
For a hungry Adam and Eve there to see.

They did not know then just what it was,
Except, that it was forbidden to eat because
The Lord forcefully ordained it and his word was law

And had to be obeyed without any exception or flaw.

In Eden, this, Adam and Eve religiously did,
Until one day a serpent, to their feet had slid.
And told them of a very special treat
If they would each of the apple eat.

First, cautious Eve and then gullible Adam took a forbidden bite,
And suddenly, what was cloudy and dull, became to them bright,
From stolen data acquired without learning and absent any insight.
Resulting in their expulsion from the Garden of Eden that night.

Be not upset, and take heed of the lessons of this biblical tale.
Follow the wise man's advice so that you won't end up in jail
And, if ignorant and living in an earthly Paradise where you wish to stay
Just ignore the old adage that: "An apple a day will keep the doctor away."

-22-

I think it's absurd not to use the adverb especially if the literati don't like it.

The Adverb

Oh no. Oh no.
Please say it isn't so.
Take it out! Take it out!
As there is no doubt
That the adverb
Is a word.
No respectful writer

Would use,
Except to be obtuse.
But the novice writer wanna-be—
Inexperienced in applied creativity—
Untrained in the ways of the literati,
Uses constantly
Dreaded adverbs
As their pet words.
And through this process
Of much excess,
It makes the clear hazy,
The exact and concise
Ambiguous and imprecise,
The story's action slowed and lazy.

I do to all of that humbly confess,
And I plead guilty to this excess.
So, I promise to you
That the penance I will do
Will be to remove from draft two
More than a few
Of those offending words,
Namely, those damn adverbs.

I will gladly swallow this bitter educational pill,
And remove the adverb in exercise of free will.
But first, before I get down to this serious biz,
Please enlighten me as to what an adverb is!

-23-

If music is the food of love, Nature's sky flyers will provide lovers with a sound romance.

The Music Of Love

Yesterday I heard a bird sing,
It was a most unusual thing.

It was not a chirp or a subdued tweet,
But still, it sounded oh so very sweet.

It played a recurring note in my memory
In sync with the concord of my history.

It is the sound of the clear blue and soft white clouded sky.
Nature's Carnegie Hall where lovers' winged-songsters fly.

It is the global stage for the majestic symphony of gentle beats,
Of warbling sounds, of songs, hums and of other sweet bleats.

Conducted vigorously by the warm and rising Sun
In a Ravel's Bolero-a repeating musical rotation.

This is one of Man's most terrible illnesses, which so far as we know, responds positively to music, but it is not known if it does the same to love. I hope it does.

Alzheimer's Man

I am a person, yes I am!
A caricature for mindless man,
Once strong of will, I had a fall.
Laid low, unable to respond or walk tall.

My mind is enveloped in a foggy cloud,
Imprisoned in a confining shroud.
Impeding my speaking of what I know.
And my understanding of what I see or hear.
My spirits are bent at their nadir low,
And my life is framed in uncharted fear.

I have unceremoniously been brought to my knees
Through the debilitating illness of Alzheimer's disease.
And in the shadow of my mind
I will, more likely than not, be all alone,
Left anonymous and undefined,
Peacefully stored in an institutional home.

I am a person, yes I am!
A caricature for mindless man,
Once strong of will, I had a fall.
Laid low, unable to respond or walk tall.

My wife and I shared an in-home office complete with computers, desks, shelves and an en-suite washroom. After I retired, she took up art as a hobby and, among other things, she also took my space in the office and called it an art studio. However, I was not upset by what I lost but rather happy that I still had something left.

Expropriation Without Compensation

I love you,
My beautiful artist true.
And your watercolours too.
You ask "So What else is new?
And why Larry, are you so blue?"

Be sure it's not because of your watercolour's hue,
Or that your artistic skills are
Too few,
Inferior or below par.

Oh no, that's not the case,
But I do feel down and dejected,
Having been unceremoniously ejected
From my computer and office space.

But I've lightened up somewhat now,
Knowing that I've escaped somehow,
From losing the one room that means so much to me—
My washroom, where I, in peace and solitude may be.

However, I know,
That the way things in my life go,
I'll also lose that room
Very surely, and soon,
As an add-on to your art studio.

Being a realistic and practical man,
I made an effective contingency plan
To address any sudden need to go,
From an unexpected prostate flow,
By buying a proper-sized tin can.

Now, the studio washroom to you I donate,
As an add-on to the studio where you create
Magnificent watercolours that are so great.
And all I ask, is your work not cease or abate
Out of any concerns as to where I'll urinate.

-26-

If Man knew the extent of what it was that he didn't know before he acted, I doubt that he would still use a common sense approach to act appropriately in respect to what he did know he knew.

Ignorance Is Not Bliss

It is true that common sense is in short supply,
Uncommonly rare and extremely hard to apply.
You can enjoy life without it and find nothing amiss,
If you live on the basis that ignorance is bliss.
And naively accept as really being true
That what you don't know can't hurt you.

But what really does go amiss,
When Man relies on ignorance
As a route to his sought-after bliss,
Is surely and most certainly this.

As Man knows not, and does not pretend
To know and cannot show
Either the beginning of or the end
Of what he does not know.
Man, in a moment of belatedly discovering life's reality,
Falls victim to *Ignorance* as its newly conversant casualty.

-27-

Mahatma Ghandi wrote of the core issues regarding *greed* as follows and I quote: "The world has enough for everyone's need, but not enough for everyone's greed." I agree.

Greed

The brain is a common and unusual tool.
Universal to Man, whether genius or fool.

It has guided him from his fundamental and suckling ages,
To his book's most sophisticated, mature and meaningful pages.

Inscribed with thoughts chronicling his feelings and emotions,
Pertaining to all of his life's worldly and important notions.

But realistically where has Man's powerful brain taken him?
Has it endowed him with a life free of immorality and sin?

Has it promoted actions of kindness, wisdom and humanity?
Has it advanced or safely secured his and other's destiny?

Has it freed him from hatred, prejudice and perpetual war?
Has it made poverty a non-existing and non-festering sore?

Unfortunately, no.
And why is that so?
Because uncontrollable human avarice and greed
Is Man's most self-destructive and poisonous seed.

Eroding away and trumping Man's spiritual and intellectual power,
To opt for the lasting good, and to forego the advantage of the hour.

-28-

Shingles are to an unlatchable latch, as an unreachable itch is to an impossible scratch.

The Shingles Patient

I hope this e-mail finds you well. If not, be sure to take your pill.
No poem today for if you are well, I do not wish to make you ill.

Instead, I advise,
If you're in bed,
It's time to rise
You're sick, not dead.

Sorry, I know that today I said no poem.
But I perceive you languishing at home,
Sadly paying for respite on your own dime,
When you can have a free groaner on mine.

As such, you should be pleased, and very happy,
That you are only getting one poem from me.
For it shows how thoughtful and timely I be,
By adhering to that truism of mine,
That a rhyme in time will save nine.

So please feel great right away,
And remain forever that way.

-29-

After fifty-six years of walking together, I finally relinquished all thoughts of ever getting ahead of her.

Come Walk With Me

Come walk with me, as we grow old,
A most intriguing time, as I am told.
A sliding downward scale of pace,
A timely sojourn from the rat race.

Come walk with me as we grow old
Still strong of mind, though not so bold.
We've earned the right to laugh and smile,
Come walk with me, to yet enjoy the while.

We resolutely lived all our yesterdays.
And proudly own our peaceful todays.
And in the interim enjoyed much fun
While making a place in the warm sun.

Now time has melded us into one,
A shared and interesting destiny
Where there's so much yet to see,
And so very much left undone.

-30-

I have a worthy adversary in the card games we play. Klubbyish is one such game. However, he can't get over losing. So I let him win because I can't stand seeing a grown man cry. He's 67 today.

The Coming Of Age

You've arrived at age sixty-seven today.
A befuddled youngster, who I must say,

Cannot make up his mind if he has retired,
Slowed down substantially, or even expired.

You certainly appear to be in limbo with your one major wish,
And that is to be able to beat me, your nemesis, at *klubbyish*.

But my advice to you is to sit back, relax and enjoy a game of fish,
As that's the only game in town that you'll be able a win to relish.

Hence, out of kindness fed by my feeling of substantial pity,
And knowing of your obsessive and compulsive personality,

Which is a cross betwixt and between sharp and witty,
As aptly defined by your friends as being mainly shitty.

I did out of pity for and kindness to you, indulge in gambling sins
By allowing you to enjoy and brag about a plethora of bogus wins.

Now, to get back as to why we are all here...
The other guys and me wish you good cheer.

And congratulate you, as only all of us really can,
On your birthday of coming of age as a young man,

And in that regard, we enthusiastically say,
Mazel tov on this your *Bar Mitzvah* day.

We note that in your life's sixty-seven year span,
It certainly took you long enough to become a man.

Glossary:
Klubbyish: is an old card game of chance.
Maz'l tov: means good luck. *Maz'l tov* is the Yiddish pronunciation for *mazel tov* in Hebrew.
Bar Mitzvah: is the religious ceremony at which a Jewish boy is recognized as a man, and takes the responsibilities of doing good deeds and is alone responsible for his actions.

-31-

Whether it be working clothes, or the emperor's clothes, it's always nice to have a complete wardrobe.

Genius And Common Sense

Ralph Waldo Emerson once expressed
That common sense is genius dressed
In its working clothes.
And, although this, I may readily admit
Is brilliantly penned with skill and imagery,
Some distortions appear because of its brevity.
For genius, as some life experiences disclose,
May show up as in the fabled Emperor's clothes,
As being entirely absent, or unable to make a fit
For those poor souls who are in dire need of it.

-32-

To experience the benefit of a free hour of legal advice while in your lawyer's office, requires you to stand up, make a complete circle to the left and then reverse your course to the right, and again making a complete circle back to where you started, no wiser but much dizzier.

The Give And Take Of Greed

I had a small fender bender and a quite minor whiplash.
A condition, if faked, would be worth some hard cash.
So I met with the local legal beagle for an hour of his free legal advice,
And while we were meeting, my injuries miraculously doubled in size.

During the free hour, he questioned me only about tombstone information,
Ignoring all my questions that would result in me getting free legal advice.
Clearly, he did not intend to give something of worth without compensation,
And I had no intentions of paying a fee for such a non-informative exercise.

The cat and mouse game
That we were playing,
Goes without saying,
Was primarily the same.

He announced that my free time was up, and gratuitously, then some,
With less than a half page of notes, he said, the clock had finally run.
I was astonished, as I learned nothing during these 60 minutes with him.
I was not even told, though I asked, as to what my chances were of a win.

He had become a tiger now and asked important questions of me.
Not the least of which was: How would I pay his $500 an hour fee?
Before I could answer, he put a written retainer in front of me to be signed,
Requiring prepayment of a $5000.00 deposit, which I promptly declined.

I told him I would read it and take it with me,
And let him know what my decision would be.
I left his office whole, as I paid him nary a penny
In return for his meaningless and worthless non-fee.

He lost an hour of productive time,
And I too wasted an hour of mine.
Yet, in the end, I truly felt great in not pursuing my phony claim,
And in depriving my would-be lawyer of his high fees for the same.

-33-

   The lessons to be learned from this sad poem are: 1) not to let your slaves become involved in your pyramid-scheme, and/or, 2) not to count on your slave keeping his finger in a hole in the dam if you can't swim.

The Original Abolitionists

Moses and Aaron asked Ramses centuries ago
To allow the Israelites enslaved in Egypt to go.
Ramses contemptuously asked: Who wants to know?
It is Yahweh, our Lord who just will not accept a no.

No way! I, mighty Pharaoh, this doth to you say,
Tell your pushy God that the Israelites will stay.
And that my Gods are much better than He is,

So hassle me not again with all this crazy biz.

God quickly responded to Pharaoh's bile,
Using the staff of Aaron to strike the Nile,
Causing the mighty river to turn blood red,
With smelly, rotting fish that were all dead.

Pharaoh spoke, Been there, seen this trick from our magicians before,
And since our sorcerers use this tired ruse, it is currently a real bore.
Tell your Lord that my answer is His people can't go.
Beat it! And if you dare to return, bring a better show.

This, Aaron and Moses knew how to do,
And brought Pharaoh something anew.
A plague of live green frogs of a million or two,
Leaving the Egyptians in gastronomical disgrace,
As nary a one of them ate frogs' legs in that place.

But, as Ramses' sorcerers could replicate frog reproduction,
Pharaoh refused to extend to the two any generous unction,
And steadfastly reiterated a positive no.
The Israelites will not be allowed to go.

This brought to Pharaoh the plagues of pestilence, pesky flies and lice,
Which for the Egyptians were very unpleasant and definitely not nice,
Leaving those denizens in pain from sores, scratching and insect bites,
Punishments not visited by Yahweh on any of His protected Israelites.

Pharaoh waivered from maybe to yes and then to no again,
And finally decided that the Israelites in Egypt will remain.
Then came the plagues of body boils, hail and millions of hungry locusts,
Bringing skin diseases, iced rains, bug-infested skies and eclipsing dusts.

That's enough! The Israelite males can leave their women here and go,
But the matzo ball and chicken soup motherly chefs are a definite no.
They will remain to prepare their Jewish penicillin delicacies just so,
For the great Egyptian people and for their most wonderful Pharaoh.

With that, the plague of darkness came upon the land and skies,
And the light of neither the sun nor moon entered Egyptian eyes,
Causing Ramses to relent and let the Israelites say their goodbyes
On condition they leave without their much-prized sheep and well fed long-horned cattle.
But Yahweh nixed this, and Ramses prepared for a rack of lamb and beef-brisket battle.

Pharaoh mocked Yahweh holding His plenary powers in full scorn,
Risking a tenth plague where Egyptians would lose their firstborn.
This plague occurred as the Lord passed through the land,
And the Egyptians' firstborn were destroyed by His hand.

Pharaoh then gave in and let the Israelites go.
They left quickly with cattle and family in tow.
While on the run, they baked tasteless, unleavened breads
In the hot sun on makeshift trays balanced on their heads.

Pharaoh reneged, and chased the Israelites toward the Red Sea,
Which parted as the Israelites arrived and crossed it in safety.
But the approaching Egyptian army, unlike Noah's son Shem,
Drowned, in an angry Red Sea that rapidly surrounded them.

So from the above we know
And the bible tells us so;-
That the Israelites' escape from the slavery of their then Egyptian host
Gave rebirth to an early vibrant culture, and reduced another to toast.

-34-

I make this recommendation even though I am fully aware that many people are regularly poked while in bed without being stabbed in the back.

My Advice To You Today

The Ides Of March is on this day again upon us.
The day poor Caesar was thrown under the bus,

And brutally stabbed in the back by the honourable Brutus,
In conspiracy with, and upon, the urging of the evil Cassius.

So beware the Ides of March, as the wise soothsayer to Caesar then said,
And take my gratuitous advice that it is better today for you to stay in bed.

-35-

Mindless is to useless, as senseless is to pulling teats on a bull.

Mindless

What is the human mind?
We talk about it every day
As though it is of a word type or kind,
That simply is, but cannot be defined,
Having too many shades of grey.

Such shades adjust as the colors of the chameleon,
Changing in order to sync with the contextual tone.
Of language's ambiguities and idiomatic usage,
Which alter or disappear with time's tutelage.

So too, the mind's essence is certainly not apparent.
Is it a non-material but thinking and learning agent?
Is it, or does it reside in, the operative human brain,
Or everywhere or nowhere in our physical frame?

But Man in the fullness of time simply could not and was unable to show
What the mysterious and deeply hidden secrets of the mind were, and so,
He in an enduring frustration concluded after all was said and done,
Man most likely was the proud owner, if not the wise user, of one.

-36-

   My friend recently returned from Israel and described the latest trend there is pay toilet boutiques, where you can rent your own throne to sit on, rule from and then abdicate, all for a few *Shekls*.

Oh Yes I Can—Israel's Toilet Boutique

Toilet to let!
Toilet to let!
But, dear tourists, think about it...
What, in the end, do you really get?

If you're in need of a can,
Whether a woman or man,
And nature urgently calls,
And you're with or without balls,
You can most certainly be sure
That you'll obtain a relieving cure
Of whizzing or of making a *drekl*,
But only if you pay a hefty *shekl*.

Yet this is so imaginatively,

And yes so typically Israeli.
A rental boutique,
Sufficiently unique,
To enjoy the after-effects of the pause that refreshes,
After only one or two energetic and effective flushes.

Glossary:
Dreckl: Yiddish slang for human solid waste.
Shekl: Slang for Israeli money;

-37-

There are many millions of true refugees in the world on the run, and the majority of them are children and women in need of help. They are all real persons, many of whom are persecuted because of their race, religion, nationality, membership in a particular group and political views, as well as for resisting the tyranny in their homeland. [*Editor's Note: Even as I have struggled with Mr. Band about punctuation in his poetry, this particular poem deserves none.*]

I Am A Person

I am a person
I definitely am
No matter what you say
I have a right to be
But you didn't see me that way
So I ran
And became a refugee

I am not just a person
I am a woman too
I have the right to be me

And to live with dignified equality
But you didn't see me that way
So I ran
And became a refugee

Without a country and without a home
I have lost my friends and family
I am depressed and desperately alone
Tortured by your tyranny

I am not merely a piece of meat
Nor am I simply State property
But you did see me that way
So I ran
And became a refugee

Oh countrymen of mine
Do what you can in time
To free our country
From the misery
And darkness of the night
Descending upon us
Through the bigotry and narrow mindedness
Of rulers intent on extinguishing our light

We cannot despair nor be afraid, my friends
Nor surrender our hope before our journey ends
Our strength resides in what we seek
Justice dignity and freedom for both the strong and weak

-38-

The persons referred to in the poem are friends I have known for over 61 years and who have been married to one another for over 50 years. He is a retired doctor, a skilled artisan and a talented writer of novels, and he will tell you that his greatest achievement was marrying his wife. She is a nurse who conquered her addiction to the cigarette.

Puff, Puff: The Magic Drag-on

She, now is only addicted to him.
Having repented her smoking sin.
She has fifty years of him under her belt,
And even so, still looks lovely and svelte.
Busy with life all the time,
And enjoying it all just fine.

How does she manage this, you may reasonably query?
How does she keep a disposition so outgoing and cheery?
That's not too difficult to explain,
For amazingly she is, in the main,
Driven by a strong and ever enduring will,
That ensures that she will her dreams fulfill.

This includes her strength of mind
To overcome whatever and every kind
Of adversity, or disheartening events,
Which, in others would cause irreparable dents.

Not her, as she has overcome problems of serious ill health
She's been there, and done that with a super-woman's stealth!
Suffered the affliction
Of tobacco addiction,
And without meaning to diminish that with a pun or joke,
That problem seems to have dissipated in a puff of smoke.

Congratulations, my dear in conquering that terribly hard habit to break,
And giving the boot to tobacco, that weed of despair and of heartache.
Remain as you are and as we enjoy and admire,
So that we, as your long-time and caring friends,
May embrace the warmth and heat of your life's fire,
And the brilliance of the light that it to us extends.

-39-

  Here, I am describing a real person except there is nothing real that I have said about him. He is an excellent golfer. Everyone likes him, and enjoys our group lunches. Indeed, he has never opted to pass up our lunch in favour of a golf outing during Canada's Winter months of November, December, January, February and March. Now that's loyalty.

The Golfer

What kind of man would rather putt
Than with his esteemed friends supp?

Truly, could you like him at all,
That man of unmitigated gall?

He's the hapless and erratic golfer who's too stubborn to switch,
From the frustration of golf to the pleasures of a deli sandwich.

So this Thursday at the eatery I had to tell all the guys,
Something I'm sure they knew, or already did surmise,

That, if the sun shines on a Thursday,
The golfer will, to our chagrin and dismay,

Deprive us of our fair-weather friend's company,
And next show on a day that is icky and rainy.

While that might be an option justified and okay...
It isn't, as our golfer doesn't know how to play.

-40-

  Toronto's Mayor Ford was a sorry politician who gave the City of Toronto notoriety founded on widespread unproven rumours of his drug and alcohol abuse and alleged criminal associations.

Goodbye, Toronto Gravy Train

I'm sorry, I'm sorry, I truly and really am.
And I'll do everything that I possibly can.
To be a public servant who's always sober,
As I am sure there is nothing nobler.
Than to be a Toronto Mayor who can act and think,
Without taking a fix or even an intoxicating drink.

And I want you to believe me when I say,
That today is the day,
And that now is the time,
When I leave behind any associates in crime.
And I'm not referring to the forty-three
Associates who serve on Council with me.

I want you to know, that by asking for a second chance,
I am not delivering to you my usual song and dance.
Instead, I seek everyone's help, support and active participation,
To help me achieve a complete and sobering election rehabilitation.

Ford nation, use your ballot and give Olivia Chow
The heave-ho, as only you are able to, and know how.
Also, I besiege you to vote against nice-guy John Tory,
Whose campaign has no plot to whatever is his story.
There's no need to mention the others at all, or by name,
As they have no agenda, or what they do have is too inane

Take heart my dear and loyal electorate, for I am back!
And I'll yet again remove the gravy train from the track!
And you can be sure that if I am once again elected,
My Scarborough friends you will not be neglected.

I promise you that my return on this most memorable day,
Will ensure the morphing of the gravy train into a subway.
And to you my dear friends, I tip my hat,
And raise my full glass and drink to that!

-41-

My friend suffers from acid reflux symptoms, which also causes his friends to suffer collateral damage.

The Gas Line

Here follows, my good friend,
A rhythmic incantation,
For a quick and immediate end
To our current aggravation,
Regarding your acid reflux,
And its very odorous efflux.

Though painful as your reflux illness may be,
You remain the master of your own destiny.
Honour your destiny and overcome reflux as you alone can...
Start by ceasing to be the freelance leftovers garbage man.

Next, push yourself away earlier from the kitchen table.
Tell anyone who'll listen to the fable of what you're able,
Including that of your super willpower to enjoy even a diet that sucks,
In order to effectively and finally get rid of that damn evil acid reflux.

Equally important to us, your dear and fine friends,
Is that all bad events will eventually come to good ends.
And, as such, that not so odourless spin-off gas
Will, with your reflux also quickly pass,
Leaving most of you in good health and well,
And all of us without that ominous smell.

-42-

I wrote a poem for a tongue-tied friend who thought he was in love or in lust. After I learned that he was too shy to send it, I gave him this.

The Love Poem

Love poems once written must
Not be allowed to collect dust.
They should immediately be sent,
Or their usefulness, as tools of lust,
Will be spent.
And you'll be a sorrowful gent.
All alone,
Holding your own.

-43-

The eleventh commandment for men whose wives play Mah Jongg is, "Thou shall not make conflicting social arrangements on maj night."

Mah Jongg

Come seven p.m. on Wednesday night,
My wife leaves home in full flight.
Summoned by the front door ringing gong,
Friends are calling her to play Mah Jongg.

Come hell or high water,
I know that I oughta,
Bring to her gambling sessions, her only obsession,
An abrupt and full-fledged cessation.

But I don't, for you can see,
I must continue to let it be,
For it is too profitable for me,
As it is like winning the lottery.

For through the workings of her good luck
She brings home her oft winnings of a buck.
Or, what's even still more nifty,
She'll win as much as two fifty!

The downside of all of this busy foregoing,
Is that my Diamond Lil will end up sowing
The seeds of despair of high level of discontent,
If she does not ultimately her winning ways repent.

As she will definitely lose out if she wins at this rate,
Demoralizing her *maj* friends until it becomes too late,
And they refuse to let her play next week or anon,
In their high stakes and friendly game of Mah Jongg.

-44-

The Greeks are wearing away their economy and are deep in the hole, while making love to the European Union countries. No one could blame those countries to insist that, in the event of further relations with the Greeks, the Greeks should at least use a Trojan.

Erosion

Constant dripping will wear away a stone.*
A refrain spoken by the Greeks in yesteryear.
Forewarned by passing time and a haunting fear
That nothing will remain but the windblown.

The ancient Greeks' most learned and greatest achievers
Were Aristotle and Socrates, their philosopher conceivers.
Though influential, they were unable to curb the Greek wild myths,
And, hence to this day, no one trusts them, even when bearing gifts.

So, though it is known that dripping water causes a stone's erosion,
Modern man has learned little from that repetitive wearing motion,
And meaninglessly, without thought, he moves his active lips,
Absent any useful ideas, and becoming life's new eroding drips.

*Greek Proverb

-45-

If you must go, here's how to leave.

Leave With A Smile

It's better to laugh than cry.
It's better to live than die.
Yet, when the time has come to say good-bye,
No tears, sad sighs, or frets,
No rues, boo hoos, or regrets,
For, the end is an exchange in kind,
Relinquishing the doubts in being for the undefined.

So, during all the while
Of your sojourn here,
Laugh, and be of good cheer...
And smile, smile, smile.

-46-

My daughter and her significant other traveled to the gang-war capital of the world in El Salvador to participate in the wedding of a friend, and then to return home safely as quickly as possible. After the wedding, and to my relief, they did not drive home from the Toronto airport on a Harley Davidson motorcycle.

An El Salvador Wedding

Oh my returning adventurers, wedding guests in El Salvador,
What was more exciting, the wedding or the ongoing gang war?
Happily, I welcome both of you home, my erstwhile travelers true,
Still in one piece, but I must say I am really nervous about you two.

As based on your recent travel history
I am sure, oh yes, I am,
That your next trip abroad will be
To attend a Bar Mitzvah of an Afghan Taliban.

-47-

  Going to Florida involves spending many moons looking for a place in the sun to rent, paying a 30% exchange rate to buy American dollars, driving two and a half days by car to get there and the same to get home. In addition, between coming and going, my wife and I each easily gain 10 to 15 lbs. by over-eating. Finally, we return home, much poorer by far than when we left Canada. In these circumstances any attack on others for rejecting such a vacation evidences a serious disconnect from reality.

Canadians Come To Florida

My spouse is her usual great
And my terrible flu did dissipate.

The weather here is 78
And rain we don't anticipate.

We urge you to come here for a warm and sunny stay
And to keep the ravages of our Canadian winters at bay.

Here, you need not suffer the freezing effects of sleet, ice or snow,
Which, in Canada, for months you'll encounter wherever you go.

So if you stay where you are during the winter to come,
You'll certainly understand why that folly is so dumb.

As enduring Canadian winter, cold as homebound moles,
Will leave you depressed and feeling like northern A-holes.

-48-

When Canada's Fall season arrives, Mother Nature, in the fullness of the beauty of this time, gives meaning to the name that Canadians use to describe that season.

Autumn's Sign

I am covered with what looks like varicose veins.
They are my sap's highways of exchange lanes.

They readily appear on my being from my stem to my stern
To aid a carbon dioxide exchange with a free oxygen burn.

Which photo-synthetically assists our dull globe to become green
And to be surrounded by beautiful blue skies, cloudless and clean.

For now, I am stem-anchored in a lofty place, riding a mild, gentle and erratic breeze
Whist soon I'll become a free-floating agent cut loose by a sap-blocking Fall freeze.

And just as I am about to expire and experience my decease
I'll morph into a plethora of colours that will the senses please.

And with Autumn's blue skies above and the brown earth beneath,
I take my leave, and gently flutter to the ground as a whirling leaf.

-49-

  I have become the recipient in my lifetime of many a strange gift from friends. Often they are imaginative tools that are used to perform specific useful tasks. Most of them have no descriptive name for the function they were designed to perform, and sometimes that can cause misunderstanding.

An Imaginative Gadget

No, it is not just a genderless playful toy.
It's useable by man, woman, girl or boy,
To get in and out of difficult and tight spots,
Without remotely giving anyone the *hots*.

It lets you securely grab and hold on to your prey quite hard,
And once you've taken that obelisk-like object internally,
You should certainly not be hung up on your own petard,
As your actions can most readily be justified morally.

It works well even though your target is long, and slippery as butter,
Relax my friend, you clearly need to get your mind out of the gutter.
Know well this poem is not intended to be at all obtuse or pornographic,
Instead, it is the expression of me, a beneficiary quite pleased and ecstatic,
With your kind gift of a mechanical pickle picker that is oh so pragmatic.

My friends often try to fit a round peg into a square hole, with the result that the jacket and shirts they sent me fit like a glove, but not like a jacket or shirt.

A Loss Due to A Gain

I must sadly and fully report,
The jacket's sleeves are too short,
And the material of the shirts are too thin or fine,
Underscoring those unruly chest nipples of mine.

Yet, worse still, the shirts cover not,
My gargantuan and protruding pot.
Although they can be altered a lot,
Unfortunately for me, I cannot.

So we have finally reached that finite limit,
As to what you and I can do to make a fit.
And the cause as to why that's so, I'm sure you'll readily understand,
As being my self-indulgent gluttony not caused by a wayward gland.

Hence, I will quickly call you
To find out what I should do
With these wonderful clothes,
Which of me, too much shows.

Much of my free time as a retired gentleman is spent at the local Second Cup Cafe enjoying excellent Java, making new friends, and discussing vacation plans as well as celebrating the execution of the same.

Barbados Bound

New friend I bid thee a joyous ado...
Yes I really do!
Even if this poem is written in a mould
That suggests that I do not!
But remember you're going where it is hot,
And I am the one remaining in the cold.

The almost jealous tone
Of this poem
Is not surprising at all.
When considering the gall
Of your surreptitious teasing,
Which was less than pleasing.

As endured by me at the Second Cup café,
When, on every other day,
I was reminded and told
By this young technocrat:
Yes, Toronto is cold,
Too bad about that.

However, as that lucky young programmer knows,
I'm pleased that he'll be living in Barbados.
Lying in the hot sun on the beach while working hard,
Trying to earn his expenses for his overly long stay there.
While this coffee drinking and retired old bard
Will have uninterrupted use of his vacant Second Cup chair.

In any event be well and *carpe diem*.
And when you return I'll see you then,
But don't come back sun baked or toasted,
As here, only the coffee beans can be roasted.

-52-

One of the most popular ways to vacation is to board a cruise ship and visit many ports along the way. My experience on a cruise has been very positive except for one aspect. Is your experience on a cruise similar?

The Ocean-Going Cruise

For breakfast, you have a tea and sizzling scone,
Half way thru the morn, a coffee and hot stone.

For lunch, you have a meal fit for hoi poi nobility,
Then a swim in the pool and a long look at the sea.

A sit on the deck in the hot sun
Then, when one side is done,

A shower, a lounge on deck on the undulating tide,
Well oiled and baking your un-tanned white side.

You laze, watching the setting sun as it descends,
And marvel how quickly a great day on deck ends.

You both dress to the nines for a floating gourmet delight,
Engage and dine at the table with the guests in the night.

And then you gracefully take leave for the after-dinner show,
One of the two remaining places where you really want to go.

After giving a standing ovation for the song and dance stable,
You're off to the casino to make your fortune at the gaming table.

If this sounds familiar to you, it probably is. You've done that and been there!
And if you are anything like me, you lost your shirt and left the ship in despair.

-53-

   My attendance at synagogue is quite rare and are entirely of a social and non-religious nature. However, once I am at the synagogue, I will try not to embarrass my family or others and so go through some of the motions as a function of respect and not of belief.

A Non-Believer's Day At the Synagogue

You ask how *shul* was today.
Really, what can I say?

My mind and body were boggled,
As I rocked back and forth and *shokld*.

All as I prayed and prayed,
And was so well behaved.

I sat and stood when everyone did that,
I wore a *kipa* in lieu of my baseball hat.

I even kissed the Torah as it went by,
Bringing a tear of joy to my wife's eye.

We came on time and held good seats where we could see and hear,
The Rabbi spoke wise words and the cantor sang so heavenly clear.

So to answer your question directly, *shul* was neat!
Especially when we went to the dining-hall to eat.

Glossary:
Shul: Yiddish for a synagogue.
Shokld: Yiddish for shook.
Kipa: Hebrew for skullcap.

-54-

I received an e-mail from an American couple who wrote me that they want to move to Canada before their country is surrounded by a Trump-built, and Mexican paid for, Wailing Wall. Also they didn't want to live in a gated community. Below is my reply to that e-mail.

An Anti-Establishment Mess

Dear Michelle and Barack:

Election of demagogue Republican leader, Donald J. Trump
Would be a Conservative kick in the American people's rump.

While on their other end, he is performing a socially destructive lobotomy,
Rewriting the Constitution, insulting minorities and destroying the economy,

Causing multiple wildly orgiastic stock market rises and falls,
Ending in a climax with China holding Americans by the balls.

So if you want to end up in a good place, not singing the blues,
Forget about Messrs. Trump, Kasich, Carson, Rubio and Cruz.

As their policies seem ambiguous, non-existent or absurd,
As well Ted may yet be a disqualified Canadian snowbird.

So who's left to be President of the U.S. of A.?
Perhaps a Democrat may be able to win the day?

But Hillary Clinton's e-mail gaffs and lack of trust issues are really bad news.
And Bernie? He can't win by pushing socialist, leftist, anti Wall Street views.

But if you and your wife really want to move to Canada, please understand and know,
You'll have to wait in line behind 25,000 new refugees, the creation of Justin Trudeau.

-55-

I so rarely get accolades or compliments for my poetry that I really appreciate the gesture and must respond.

A Swelling Of The Head

Thank you so much for giving me a huge swelled head.
But now I wonder and must ask this from what you said.
Which of the two should I more readily prize,
My brain or backside, now of the same-size.
Though I sit on one more often than I exercise my brain.
Yet, the by-product of both appears to everyone, the same.

Every Friday evening, eight residents at our condominium, including my wife and I, have a standing dinner date to dine out. Unfortunately, on one such night my wife was sick and could not attend, so I sent regrets on our behalf.

Ms. Sheila Regrets She's Unable To Attend

Oh sadness and pestilence,
We bemoan our absence.
But we are A.W.O.L. with clear conscience.
Relying on true and tried medical prudence,
And good old-fashioned common sense,
Indicating that Sheila is yet in her early convalescence.
Feeling out of sorts and missing her usual effervescence,
As well as some of her lively luminescence and luxuriance.
She, without any malevolence or pretence,
Resists, based on sound altruistic influence,
To make any unnecessary public attendance
Until she recoups her earlier healthy resilience.

So although we'll miss dining with all of you, there is a spin-off compensating blessing...
Namely as Sheila is almost well, and yet abed, I could for dessert, enjoy some messing.

-57-

My friend and wanna-be-lawyer, defended himself from a parking ticket charge, researched the law and argued as his main defense a Charter violation and miracle of miracles, he won.

Justice In Traffic Court

I do extend my congratulations to you
For having the guts, and brainpower too,
To do on your very own,
While standing all alone,
Before a judge who could easily have fined you, and thrown you under the bus,
But refrained from doing so, as he did not know, what the hell the Charter was.

Yet in the end, justice appears to have been done,
Even if a known wrongdoer beat the rap, and won.
You excelled in protecting your rights so skilfully and so expertly...
That when I next get in trouble, I'll be sure to have you represent me.

-58-

Sometimes, a play on words, in more than one language, with more than one meaning, can be much fun...as well as very confusing.

Neither Here, Nor There—Neither Hen, Nor Hare

My mind and body somehow don't seem to meld.
Have I already passed on, and gone to *yener velt*?

I doubt it, for I believe, although not too certain,
That no one as yet, has rung down my curtain.

So probably, though not entirely clear,
If I am not gone, I must still be here.

And as to where I fit in, I now with you will happily share.
I am oft described in Yiddish, as *"nisht ahin un nisht aher."*

In English that clearly means, "I am, neither here nor there."
And that does not translate into me being a hen, a rabbit or a hare.

Even though *"ahin"* has the dual meaning of "here" and a "hen,"
And *"aher"* means "there," and is not a misspelling for "a hare."

Yet those critters describe me conversely in every way.
The hen with its propensities always enjoys a good lay.

The promiscuous rabbit or hare enjoys a multiple sexual score,
All of which, I truly and sadly admit I am unable to do any more.

-59-

Despite the high cost of living in London, my friends returned from vacation there with twenty English pounds.

English Bob, or Kabob

If you returned with some of that with which you went,
That extra dividend is not likely to be god sent.
And so, I hope that those twenty extra pounds,
That you told me about are English currency,
And not what happens when on a diet truancy.
Although I must admit that, to me, it sounds
Like you pigged out and devoured a glutton's fillings,
And came home with many more pounds than shillings.

-60-

The measure of man cannot be determined by measuring tape.

In Praise Of The Measure Of Man

Dear friend, please don't feel distress
When you hear your wife express,
"Oh such *ha-penis*! Such *ha-penis*!"

She is not exuding or expressing sexual joy,
But lamenting at the smallness of your toy!

Alleging that it's just like you, a perpetual softy,
Once standing tall, erect and certainly very lofty.

But now, at age 83, your self-lauded ardour and libido are sadly all done,
And that's not surprising, as you changed from having one to being one.

-61-

A friend told me that August 2015 has five Saturdays and five Sundays according to the Chinese claendar. This happens once every 823 years, and when it does, if you tell your friends about it, and your Feng Shui is right, you'll receive a pocket full of money. Hence the event is called Silver Pocket Full. I penned the poem below on the promise that my friend (a fantastic cook and baker) would send me a blueberry flan if I did. I did, and she did.

The Chinese Silver Pocket Full

There's certainly no need for me to become mired
In the idiosyncrasies inherent in a calendar of the Chinese.
For I enjoy as many Sundays in a month as I may please,
And that's the way it is, simply because I am retired.

In order to wait for 823 years for a *Silver Pockets Full* arrival,
I'll have to be healthy to support such a very lengthy survival.
My life-style throughout will have to be quite pure and pristine,
Untainted by any self-indulgence in American Chinese cuisine.

Further, I do not embrace the theory of Tao's way,
Nor do I pay much attention to what Confucius say.
I am in harmony with my environment as per Feng Shui,
As I do whatever I want, so long as my mind says it's okay.

So I'll ignore the esoteric oriental calendar stuff.
Be a more than lucky, happy and well-fed man.
And, will definitely have more than is enough,
If I get five Sundays monthly of your blueberry flan.

-62-

The lighthouse light of my love pulsates and shines in sync with the beam and beat of my heart, and we are and remain as one.

My Lighthouse

In the deepest recesses of my heart,
Lodged there with a smile, and full of kindness,
Resides a vital and most precious part,
Without which, and absent such quintessence,
Life for me
Would be
A circumscribed, meaningless pretence.

She is my own, my very own,
Her heart, her smile, her laugh, my home.

No meanness flaws her.
No hatred gnaws her.

Engrossed in spirit and in form,
As wife and mother,
Friend and lover,
All superbly high, above the norm.

She is my luminescent and my guiding lighthouse beam,
Shining brightly to highlight all the realities of my dream.
Always beautifully aglow, when on rough seas or on calm shore.
She is the light of my life and I certainly could not love her more.

-63-

   A pet peeve of mine is the confusion of meanings that exist in the use of the English language. There are multiple English words having the same, and/or different meanings even though their sounds, and/or spellings may be the same or different.

Complement, Or Compliment

Is it compliment or is it complement?
The "i" and "e" make them different.
When I receive the former, my head swells and quickly my ego grows.
And the latter, harmonizes the myth from which the compliment flows.

-64-

My friend just underwent his second knee operation on the same leg, and I sent this poem to him just after this operation to make him feel better.

What A Nice Old Man

You just completed knee operation two,
And soon you'll be as good as new.
Making you worth, at least times two.
No, for sure you will think it's more...
Something like, good old you, times four.

But since they operated twice on one knee,
It'll probably be only you times three.
But whatever we fix the multiple at,
We happily praise you and doff our hat,

For not being a complaining and miserable old wretch,
Even now while moving through to the home stretch.
So we ask and expect you to be brave and keep a stiff upper lip,
As for sure, nothing else can fit that bill anywhere near your hip.

-65-

Why the word "host" is an integral part of the word "hostage."

Toronto, The Pan Am Gamester

Anywhere you go
In the city of Toronto,
By subway or by auto,

You can reasonably anticipate
That you will at least be late,
Or more likely, a no show.

As that was the way it always was,
Even if you took a taxi or a city bus,
Or cycled on your trusty bike,
Or jogged, or just took a hike.
Now, there is a much worse traffic jam,
As Toronto has bought into the Pan Am.

It's not that bad we hear our tourists say,
But that is only true, if one has all day.
To idle one's car beside the useless HOV lane,
While going to work or to the Blue Jay's game.
The politicians puff that the games will make our tourists happy and hyper.
So what's our benefit, it's not the tourists, but us who have to pay the piper.

-66-

If your image is captured and frozen in time by a picture, and if years later, you look into the looking glass of time, which, if any, image of you is reality.

Of Smoke And Mirrors

I gaze into the mirror and see now, what never was there.
It is my reflected image, replicated to my very last hair.
However, how do I know for sure the image is real and true?
And the handsome and smiling reflection is me, and not you.

As I have never ever been
On my other side, looking in.

I am wary of the photo, as it is of no assist,
And so for sure my real doubts will persist
As the camera's obtuse angles and poor light often lie
When forcing an image through a grounded lens' eye.
So when I look into the mirror, what in reality do I see?
I see not reality at all, but the distortion time makes us be.

I have some pictures of my bride and me taken some 50 years ago.
She is still she, and I am me, but that's not what the pictures show.
I compare their images to those I now see in the mirror,
Very much surprised, and, I withdraw in utter horror.
As I do now clearly and most certainly see
How badly a mirror does distort one's reality.

-67-

My chum and his wife stayed with us in a hotel near Niagara-on-the-Lake. He loves to eat and I think what he saw when we were in the hotel's Gazebo made him jealous.

Canadian Ground Hogs

I sure am enjoying the bright morning sun,
Seated on the Gazebo's bench having fun,
Watching two creatures in the grassy common,
A pair of clumsy, rotund Canadian groundhogs,
Sunning themselves on fallen, moss-covered logs.

Slowly, they crawl into the field along the low-lying grasses,
With heads down and dragging their enormous tailless asses.

Moving hither and thither, seemingly without a care.
And randomly nibbling away on leafy and grassy greens,
Which, at a quick glance and at first appearance seems
To be a table set for them of an endless gourmet fare.

The serenity of the moment is suddenly shaken,
And the silence in the gazebo is quickly taken
By my friend, a third truly Canadian hungry hog,
A known gourmet and worshiper of the hot dog.

Although it was morning and about just ten past nine,
He had his FREE hotel breakfast for the third time.
Now seated he watched the hogs eat until he could stand it no more,
And quickly, he left the gazebo, for FREE breakfast number four.

So, my dear ravenous and perpetually hungry friend...
Let my light verse to you precisely and clearly portend,
That if you continue to compete with or mimic the Canadian ground hog,
Then you will present mostly as an uncomfortable rotund bump on a log.
And if you over-indulge and over-eat,
You will find it's really not so neat,
To have an over-sized tailless seat.

-68-

There is a good reason why my kids gave me a license plate that asks, "Where am I?" However, for the same reason it could have asked, "Where am I going?" And here's why.

An Unforgettable Get Together

It's seven o'clock and it's getting late,
But at my age, it's hard to appreciate

And understand, yes late, but for what?
Oh sometimes, I'm such a forgetful nut.

Really, where am I supposed to go?
It may be Chicago or perhaps Buffalo.
More important, am I going with somebody?
Who I am supposed to meet in the lobby?

It is to me a big uncertainty,
A real confounding mystery.
As maybe, I'm supposed to be
Meeting all of them at the Deli.

I feel like such a darn and ungodly fool,
So maybe I'm going with the rabbi to shul.
Or am I going to play a game of 10-card gin,
And suffer another payless and pyrrhic win?

I notice from what is writ in my trusty diary's log,
On the morrow the gourmets and I go for a hot dog.
I know, as I stand before the mirror and brush my white hair,
That I'm supposed to be some place, but I don't know where!

Should I wake my wife, my sleeping beauty,
To ask her if something is doing at nine-thirty?
No, she's having too nice and sound a sleep-in.
To wake her now would be such a cardinal sin.

I'll wake her at about ten...
And probably by then,
I may hear from the tight-assed upset, Morgenshteen,
That they're waiting for me in their Hyundai machine.

-69-

I had no idea that the penguin, a bird that cannot fly and is black and white, has 50 shades of grey reasons for not flying.

Why Penguins Don't Fly

A penguin looks so damn abnormal,
As it's always dressed to the nines,
Decked out in its tux at all times,
And looking so cute and adorable.

Yet the penguins, have often been accurately described,
As sexually prolific birds populating the Antarctic space
And reproducing their species at a most dizzying pace,
Doing what comes naturally in the snowy and icy outside.

Indeed, their prodigious sexual appetite
Is reason why they don't fly, or fly right...
As there is no real need for it to be aloft or air bound,
Given the ample cool space to copulate on the ground.

So praise the penguin, so well dressed in its tuxedo,
As it is working the north with its impressive libido.
Moving promiscuously from mate to mate, as a fickle,
Cute and adorably active, reproductive Antarctic icicle.

-70-

Will we ever be able to overcome our history and our nature?

Unchanging

One mind is insufficient in number and kind.

One heart unable to ease the grief left behind.

The former fails Man's conundrums to ease,
And the latter bears not his soul to peace.

Can man now step out from this historical abyss,
And live an altered life, which has never been his?

Can he change from war hawk to a peaceful dove?
From an all-consuming fierceness? To gentle love?

Can the seasons no longer change? Can the winds no longer blow?
Can the earth cease to green? Can the raging rivers cease to flow?

No!
And so,

Not in this millennium will Man any reprieve win,
As he is too mired and engrossed in his own sin.

-71-

   Trees are the creation of Mother Nature that I enjoy the most, and my friend just couldn't resist taking a whack at trying to water down my love for the tree.

Trees

The tree stands universally strong and tall in its majestic essence,
A clear indication of Mother Nature's wisdom and common sense.
Its woody presence, well sculptured and dressed in bright leafy clothes,
Is sprinkled with heavenly nectar from the clouds as it upward grows.

And, as it is drawn to the bosom of the warming sun and its bright light,

It breathes life-refreshing photo synthetically every day and every night.
And, in the extreme heat of the noonday sun, it gives ample aid,
By providing a breezy umbrella of protective and cooling shade.
And, in the context of the freezing and miserable clime of a wintry zone,
It provides firewood for warmth, and lumber to build a log cabin home.

The tree, as you can readily see,
Is Mother Nature's most utilitarian gift made to Mankind.
And, if we imprudently cause its utility to be undermined,
We will very soon be
Living a life of misery.

As food that the farmer cultivates and grows
Will, without any trees be, as everyone knows,
Lost through the harsh winds and dried out breeze,
With the passing of trees into environmental absentees.

If thusly, the balance of nature is upset,
You may for sure your bottom dollar bet,
That if by Man's hands, the trees are no more,
Mother Nature will be sure to even the score.

Dear Poet Larry-Eh,

The Downside To Trees

There is a downside to certain trees,
When they cause me to sneeze and wheeze.
Their pollen spreads with each gentle breeze,
Gleefully climbing into my nose,
Causing my breathing passages to close.
So what good is that f*cking tree,
If I am dead, and can no longer see?
Most trees are good, I will admit,

But some are just not worth sh*t.
"Which ones are they?" You will query.
They are the deadly olive, and fruitless mulberry.
So enjoy your trees my poetic friend,
As long as they do not cause my untimely end.

Sincerely,
(*name withheld*)

Dear Friend,

Wrong Again—There Is No Downside To Trees

It's not the gentle and lovely tree
That causes you so much misery.
It's not the hated airborne pollen
That's making you feel so solemn.

So this I sympathetically to you propose,
What every good plastic surgeon knows,
You'd have much more relief if your nose
Were a much smaller intake hose.

Sincerely,
Poet Larry-Eh

-72-

I know that everyone who is around to enjoy another of their birthdays understands that, although they are getting older, birthdays are to be greeted with joy, and are times of celebration.

Birthday Greetings To A Friend

Age is in the mind of the be-older set.
Rest easy, as you are nowhere there yet.
You've just reached the big six-oh,
And have still a long way yet to go.

But it's better than not to grow older,
Even though
We all know,
That our feet will get flatter and colder.
Our eyesight will begin to dim,
And, horror of horrors, we'll cease being slim.

Our appetites will grow,
As our hair turns to snow.
And all the while, our waist,
With astonishing haste,
Will turn into waste.

But you, our junior birthday girl,
A much- prized oyster's pearl,
Remain a rose among the thorns,
A devilish delight without horns.

You have a lively spirit and a real love of life.
You are a good friend, daughter, mother and wife,
A most understanding and knowledgeable seer.
Content in growing older and happy to be here.

Remember that growing older is not a crime,
And there is no penalty for killing time.
We happily celebrate its inevitable passing once a year
By remembering our birth date with joy and good cheer,
And counting our many blessings and godsends,
Along with best wishes from all of your close friends.

-73-

By profession, he was a plastic surgeon and by hobby, he is a craftsman and maker of pepper mills, and an excellent novelist. I was by profession, a lawyer and a judicial officer. In real life, we are retired and the remnants of two careers and we never ceased being friends.

Two Careers

It is so grand to be retired like the two of us.
No one cares if we rant some, and then fuss.

You can write a book, whittle a mill and solve a Sudoku puzzle
I can pen an original poem, wit-a-little, and still be quite civil.

But, anything useful that we ever did,
Our lights, under a bushel, we hid.

You, a plastic surgeon, honing your skills with Botox.
I, advocating in a convoluted and legalistic context.

You, a sculpture of the Roman nose and sensuous hips.
I, a courtroom gunfighter, shooting from both of my lips.

You expanded the female chest from berries to melons.
I represented greedy losers, charlatans and near felons.

You made the aging Miss Dracula look hot and cute.
And I brought to court her most recent alimony suit.

And thusly, it proceeded for this professional pair,
Until each of us finally lost full heads of our hair.

Now neither of us is working anywhere.
As you tired of it all, and I ran out of hot air.

So now, we roll up our sleeves and forget all this crap,
By jumping into the sack for our late afternoon nap.

-74-

Geitel, my sister, was then as a young woman, and still is at 87, one of the most beautiful women I have ever had the pleasure of knowing.

My Beautiful Sister

There is nothing as wonderful as an older *shvester*,
For a much younger brother to harass and pester.
"Older" is the key.
That was my entry,
In causing sis a life of ersatz misery.

Nine years is the time that separates our age
But who's counting, so let's turn the page.

She learned very early that her beauty meant a lot,
That a slim waist beat a protruding, outgoing pot.
That a smile with even and white glowing teeth,
With a warm and charming personality beneath,
Were all very important and meaningful to possess.

But insufficient to avoid brotherly induced distress.

That came mainly in a package called me...
Yours truly, her nemesis brother, Larry!
I was what every older and beautiful sister hates.
Babysitting for a brat, who ruined most of her dates.

Indeed, until the happy day I came along,
Something at home felt terribly wrong.
As numbers, one and two for mom and dad
Were two girls whose arrivals went unrewarded.

But, when my arrival was happily and duly reported,
Then *Avrum*, our father, finally an only son had.
And happily upon our productive mother did extol,
A hard-earned well-deserved and beautiful fox stole.

In this context *Geitel,* I never said it once, or at all,
That Daddy loved me better than you.
It was more like a hundred times, as I now recall,
But, then that was only so, because it was true.

However, and notwithstanding the passage of time,
You're still pissed off, but not because of the attitude of pop,
But because you believe that I've committed the ultimate crime,
Of my legs, unlike yours, coming together beautifully at the top.

Glossary:
Shvester: Sister in Yiddish.
Avrum: The name Abraham in Yiddish.
Geitel: The name Gerry in Yiddish.

-75-

I have a relative who is a lawyer and wanna-be poetry critic, who thought I should go back to practicing law as I obviously had too much time on my hands writing poetry. He's probably right. [*Editor's Note: As I continue to deal with Mr. Band's poetic ramblings, I would like to remind him that there is, indeed, billable time in poetry—mine!*]

There's No Billable Time For Poetry

I read what you had to say,
Five weeks ago to the day.
What you wrote in your letter,
Announcing that my prose
Were very much better,
Than my poor rhyming odes.

So, to answer what your off-base comment shows,
And to expound what instinctively everyone knows,
That an Insurance lawyer and knowledge of the arts,
Alas twin as the saying goes,
Like holy rollers and promiscuous tarts.

A lawyer who claims that he has no time on his hands,
Is too busy trying to collect his fee for service demands.
Reflecting his billings of exorbitant and fictitious billable time,
That move the cost of Justice from the ridiculous to the sublime.

Finally, my delightful and young legal whiz...
Continue working your time-consuming biz.
Me? I enjoy having too much time on my hands.
Because I can stop and smell the red roses,
And contemplate the problems life poses,
While dispensing with ridiculous legal chitchat
Based on the maxim, *de minimus lex non-curat.*

Glossary:

De minimus lex non-curat is a Latin phrase meaning, "The law does not take account of small matters."

-76-

   A hot dog with beans just isn't my cup of tea, nor come to think of it, neither is tea.

Ugh! A Hot Dog With Beans

A hot dog with beans?
That to me just seems
To be an unmitigated waste
For my trim and tiny waist,
And an insult to my taste.

Surely, as a gourmet I will be undone
If I indulge in a hot dog without a bun.
Therefore, from those powerful beans, I will happily abstain,
Freeing myself from all and any odorous or noisy refrain.

-77-

   My wife, aside from having been and being an excellent teacher, interior designer, watercolour artist, pianist, mother, wife and grandmother, is also one hell of a cook.

Not A Trifling Matter

Gee whiz and holy cow!
I've devoured it all now.
And on that very deplorable and unhappy score,
Sheila, my very lovely and gastronomic saviour,
I seek an abundant and delicious trifle encore,
But if I must, I will settle for just a trifle more.

-78-

I believe that a kindred soul is that person who you love and with whom you want to share your life in a meaningfully and reciprocal way. My kindred soul is my wife.

Kindred Souls

In life to be true, you see,
I must inexorably be me.

Just as you must be you,
To do what you do.

Together, and as such,
We enjoy very much.

Living life's bounty as kindred souls,
Unspoiled by any conflicting poles.

Yet, attracted as compatible opposites,
Drawn together as matched composites.

We grow in closely connected singularity,
And experiencing peaceful conjugal parity.

Not sweating the small things, and minimizing strife,
We engage a fully serene, fun-filled and exciting life.

-79-

The "Hi-Ho Silver...Away," of Greek mythology.

Pegasus II

Pegasus, as fable has it, you were born, and started your exciting journey
With a beheaded mother's blood churning in the surf of the angry sea.

A mysteriously winged-horse hero of ancient lore and Greek Mythology,
Born of Poseidon, slyly posed as a horse to seduce Medusa, his wife to be.

Oh Pegasus, of great Hellenic myth and ancient design.
Oh winged-stallion and fabulously magnificent equine.

So strong, so pure, so wholesome, never obtuse nor tainted by rouses,
A fit and talented legend beloved by, and living with the gentle muses.

On Mount Helicon where you dug with your hooves without hesitation,
Many magnificent fountains for the charming artistic muses' inspiration.

Summoned by Zeus to his Godly, heavenly Mount Olympus home,
You there to him pledged obedience while on his lyceum throne.

And lived the rest of your life in the open heavenly Olympic sky,
Remaining there today as a constellation where you continue to fly.

So ends the fable of Pegasus and Zeus of Greek Mythology,
Heroic forerunners of the values and lore of Western Society.

Predecessor of the comic book classic read,
Of the Old Wests *yippee-kai-yai* danger,
Of Silver, the beautiful white speedy steed,
And of his masked-rider, the Lone Ranger.

-80-

I have taken this time to praise a friend in a like manner and fashion as he praises me. From what follows, it is easy to see that we belong to a mutual admiration society.

Friendship

I to you, my very good friend, here and now do homage pay,
And sing your praise before I forget what it was I had to say.

Moreover, I will do my best to let everyone know
Of your many attributes, from your head to your toe.

So, starting in front and quite high above,
Is a face that only a mother could love.

Or maybe a person whose taste is quite inane,
Or only a person carrying a long white cane.

More often than not, all your assets have left me moderately uninspired,
As though you were operating on three of five cylinders that actually fired.

For example: the weakest, least used and most isolated of your body parts,

Is cranially bound and the source of your perceived absence of the smarts.

And, the one anomaly in your being, that elevates you to an admirable creature of real class,
Is a backside, longitudinally cracked, which still allows you to be designated as a perfect ass.

To be fair, I must admit to you truly that I clearly am far from perfection too.
But, interestingly enough no one notices that, when I am standing next to you.

And now, as I finish my kind dissertation, I will cease to speak,
As soon as I figure out how to get my tongue out of my cheek.

-81-

This poem is based on many of the true circumstances as portrayed in the story of Philomena Lee, a young unwed mother who gave birth to a son in Ireland. Her son was taken from her against her will while at a Catholic institution, and put up for adoption in very sad circumstances.

Philomena

Philomena Lee did not abandon her son in infancy.
No. It was clearly God's so-called earthly agency,
Who ordained that an imposed separation must be
Mother and child's joint and unwanted destiny.

In Ireland, she gave birth to Anthony Lee.
He was her young son, who at age of three,
Was unceremoniously, and quite surreptitiously,

Separated from his mother at Sean Ross Abbey.

Through the conduct of obedient Nuns acting on dubious authority,
And without Philomena's consent to the adoption of Anthony,
He was taken from her, sent to an unknown and distant American family,
While she remained indentured to the Abbey, working in its laundry.

Philomena paid to the Abbey her out-of-wedlock dues,
And departed from the Convent and its cruel abuse.
She sought in the fullness of time to find her son using powerful ecclesiastic avenues,
Invoking their help and seeking humanitarian relief on principled Christian values.

For over 50 years her efforts to re-unite with her son failed,
As the cruelty of secrecy and silence in adoption prevailed.
Anthony's efforts too resulted in his not learning the truth of it all,
Due largely to the existence of an unholy and conspiratorial stall.

Anthony desperately wanted to be with Philomena re-united.
And three times, he visited the Abbey and desperately tried
To find her, but the Nuns, each time kept silent and continued to hide the facts until he died,
Ignorant that Philomena truly loved him, was searching for him and wanted him at her side.

Philomena's story provides bright beacons of light,
Demonstrating to Irish denizens governed by Dublin
The urgent need to legislate transparency law rights.
To defeat the evils of institutionalized manufactured sin,
So that lost children may know and embrace their origin.

-82-

Retirement allowed an old work horse like me to no longer need to busy myself with the work of business, but to engage fully with my family and enjoy the pleasure of being with them and understanding better who they are, where they are coming from and what they are capable of doing.

Retirement

Retirement is the playground of my mind,
Where I can think thoughts of every kind.

But most importantly retirement is
Nothing more and nothing less than this...

A time to stroll leisurely through the recent past,
A time to relish those pleasant memories that last.

A time when my aging body requires a little more rest,
And an afternoon nap that recharges my batteries best.

A time to better understand and enjoy my wonderful wife,
And to appreciate the fulfillment she brings to my happy life.

A time to know that my three robust, intelligent and happy children
Are not simply an extension of, but an improvement on, what I am.

A time for hearing, seeing and happily recognizing,
An equal advancement of the offspring of our offspring.

A time to eat in, or to dine out.
A time to mix and party about.

A time to enjoy all family and friends.
A time to make peace and emends.

And sadly, a time to endure
Whatever pain we can't cure.

A time to visit, to travel and to participate in life's excitement and fun.
A time to continue to discover what, if anything, is new under the sun.

A time to pass the day painting, writing, or reading a good book.
Or, better still, to learn how to draw, or to be an excellent cook.

A time to swim, to curl, or to play a leisurely round of eighteen.
A time simply to relax and to play. A time to see and to be seen.

A time to be and remain, if you can,
A competitively keen athletic man.

A time to advance the growth of our society.
A time to volunteer services to a favourite charity.

A time to do something worthwhile and good,
And, if you are willing to do all of the above,
Life in retirement will be more easily understood.
And certainly will be something you'll readily love.

-83-

I have often wondered if there are any human feelings that are more deeply felt than those born out of the mother and daughter relationship.

The Love Of A Daughter And Mother

The love by and for a mother
For and by her daughter,
Is unlike any other.
Its origins embrace the miracle of birth.
Enhanced by family values and personal worth.
It is culturally and generationally exhibited,

Freely expressed and otherwise unlimited.

Oh daughter, as every fibre of your being demonstrates,
Your love for your beautiful and gentle mother replicates
Her ever caring and enduring love for you,
Thus creating innately strong and binding glue,
Joining deep feelings so mutual, essential and true,
And bringing much happiness to the both of you.

Although your mother is no longer physically here,
The warmth of her heart and of your memories clear,
Will déjà vu the good times with her of yesteryear,
And leave her indelibly and forever spiritually near.

Then, you'll instinctively know,
Your mutual love will continue to be,
And grow.
As an uninterrupted and perpetual journey,
That has a beginning but never is done.
A most fulfilling and enchanting trip,
That moved from an earthly relationship
To that of an ethereal and spiritual one.

-84-

I have always believed that substance is more important than form

So What If I Can't Spell

Don't worry about my spelling,
There's naught in it that's telling.
Precision in artistic verse
Is most certainly perverse.

And to me makes no sense,
As I have poetic license.

-85-

After a discussion with two female friends, who insisted that dairy cows are able to give gallons of milk without having previously given birth to a calf, I penned this poem in rebuttal. I would have answered differently than with a poem, but I like milking, if not a cow then at least a joke.

When Can Cows Give Milk?

A useful animal is the gentle and fertile cow.
More so by far, than the unclean, porky sow.
As the beginnings of curds and whey, milk and butters,
Start with massaging and manipulating of their udders,
Using a repeated combination of a push, a squeeze and a pull,
But of course, only after she's been knocked up by a horny bull.

-86-

If gold is yellow money, and money talks, can silence ever be golden.

Is Silence Golden?

It is often said that silence is golden.
But that's not an adage I am sold on.

Silence is the mind's voice intentionally stilled.
Leaving hopes and wishful dreams unfulfilled.

Silence, as duly and cautiously noted,
Is rarely, if ever, authoritatively quoted.

Silence is to action as are thorny juggernauts
To the muting of useful ideas and thoughts.

Thus, if silence is golden as sages have oft extolled,
Its shimmer and glimmer is the sheen of fools' gold.

-87-

William Blake's famous poem *The Tiger*, so inspired me that I wrote the poem *The Fire Fly* which no doubt will cause him to turn in his grave and to now be known as William Bleak.

The Firefly

Firefly, firefly, glowing in the shadow of the night,
Glimmering bleakly with dim and flashing taillight.
What creator or eternal power fashioned you and why?
As you appear to be Nature's design, gone sadly awry.

A flying lantern giving no soothing light or heat
Except for the inefficiencies coming from your seat.
All of this oddity make it fair game to ask:
Are you up to any practical or useful task?

Oh firefly, oh firefly, please be honest and true,
And explain clearly what is the meaning of all this.
And why is it that every time we glance at you,
There appears to be something terribly amiss?

Did She who made the rack of lamb,
And created the butt and shank of ham.
Have anything to do
With creating you?

If your answer is an undeniable "yes,"
Then, as you are your creator's mess,
Is it reasonable to assume without harbouring malice, or being obtuse,
That your creator did all of this to you, intent on cooking your goose?

-88-

Over the ages, both hope and prayer were, and still are, used as the tools of religious men as a means of saving Mankind in difficult times. Has it worked?

Hope And Pray

What is the difference, you ask, between *to pray* and *to hope*?
This answer is given now, prior to any consultation with the Pope.

But I have today consulted my clairvoyant soothsayer
Who explained that the upshot of *to pray* is a prayer.

And a prayer is a humble request or entreaty
To an all-powerful and most beneficent deity.

Hope is the reasonable expectation that what one prays for will come to be,
And if it does, may for some, be proof enough for the existence of their deity.

But what if, as so often happens, prayers are unanswered and hopes are dashed?
Would that not reduce the deity to a figment of an imagination that has crashed?

No, for if one believes, then he has no need for proof that his deity exists.
But if one acts only on proof, its absence may create a doubt that persists.

Neither is mistaken, and none are fools.
They're just using different kinds of tools.

One is playing the odds.
The other is playing...the Gods.

-89-

A short article of mixed prose and poetry.

Oh Costco! Oh Costco!

In September of 2011, our wives learned that the Costco hot dog, then being served at the Woodbine warehouse store, was no longer deep red in color but was almost pink and also was quite soggy. They went to management to complain, not so much because they were concerned about our best interests, but because they feared that if we didn't like those hot dogs, our Gourmet Club wouldn't go to Costco's store on Thursdays and they would have to put up with us at home.

They told us about the change in the hot dog and about their complaint and we filed a written formal complaint. Costco responded quickly and efficiently. One of their managers contacted me by phone and told me that they would be looking into the problem the next morning. They did, and that afternoon called me and reported that the problem was not with the hot dog, but with how they were then being processed.

They told me that they solved the color and sogginess problem by using steamers instead of trays of water to keep the hot dogs at the required temperature and moisture consistency, while waiting to be served to the customer. They also invited the four of us to taste test the hot dogs as properly processed, so we did. We were satisfied that they did indeed solve the problem.

The four of us are professional people with over 300 years of combined and varied experience amongst us, and we were very impressed by the efficiency of Costco in addressing the concerns of their customers.

Our original complaint was in both prose and poetry, as was our final report to Costco after completing our taste-test. We send kudos to Costco and its representatives!

A. Letter of Complaint in Prose

Costco Ltd.
Woodbine Ave.
Ontario, Canada
Att: [name redacted] Food Manager
September 22, 2011.

Dear Sir;

We are a small social club of four men each over 75 years of age, who meet regularly at the Woodbine Ave. Costco's store. We call our club among other things, the Gourmet Club.

We are fans of the way Costco conducts its business and are regular patrons. We shop at Costco stores with confidence that we will receive quality and value for our money. We really have no complaints except for the one which is contained in this letter and in our enclosed 'poem' concerning our disappointment at Costco replacing a terrific food product(the hot dog) on two occasions for what appeared to be a not as good looking or tasting hot dog.

I am talking about the hot dog served as ready to eat in your fast food section at the Store at Woodbine Ave. At first, you had a very high quality and delicious brand of hot dog, which I believe, was the Hebrew National hot dog. That was changed without notice for a different brand, which was still very good. I do not remember the new brand's name but it was a good hot dog.

Then came the most recent unannounced change of hot dog, which was still a good all beef hot dog, but in our members' opinions, did not for some reason taste as good to us. It did not have the usual reddish color and seemed soggy. Concurrently with the advent of this hot dog, I believe Costco dropped the price of such hot dog by fifty cents.

Your customers in our view were satisfied with the two earlier brands and I am sure thought your price was just fine, and it was. We are disappointed about the change in taste and color of the current hot dog, and hopefully our enclosed poem says enough to the powers-that-be to consider correcting the situation. As for the poem enclosed, many a true word is said in jest.

Would you please forward this letter and poem enclosure to the head-office hierarchy at Costco for their review. Please treat this letter as a complaint to which we respectfully seek a timely response from Costco.

Lawrence L. Band. [*phone number redacted*]
(poem enclosed).

B. Complaint in Poetry

Laments from Four Gents

Oh Costco! Oh Costco!
Everyone knows;
How your hot dog goes,

So goes Costco.
Oh Costco! Oh Costco!

We four men
Every now and then
Attend at Costco's, Woodbine
For our gourmet dine
Which was just fine
Until of late
When your new hot dog we ate.

Oh Costco! Oh Costco!
Everyone knows;
How your hot dog goes,
So goes Costco.
Oh Costco! Oh Costco!

We've had your fries galore
Unchanged and to die for.
We've had many a delicious slice
Of your unvarying pizza, so nice!
Your new salad is great
So many a bowl-full we ate.

And oh yes your smoked meat
Is hard to beat,
No joke,
Goes well with the free coke
But yet
Our club members are upset.
As something is amiss, with your hot dog in a bun,
It's too moist and too pink and eating it is no fun.

Oh Costco! Oh Costco!
Everyone knows;

How your hot dog goes,
So goes Costco.
Oh Costco! Oh Costco!

So please replicate your hot dogs' quality taste of yore,
As the new ones do not taste quite as good as before.
We don't think you intended such a negative change
But these wieners aren't in as good or an acceptable taste range
So please investigate our complaint quickly and earnestly
And hopefully it'll be easy to restore the hot dogs' taste quality.

Oh Costco! Oh Costco!
Everyone knows;
How your hot dog goes,
So goes Costco.
Oh Costco! Oh Costco!

Have a nice day
Yours truly
Me
Poet Larry-Eh

C. Our Prose Report on our Taste-Test of the Hot Dog

September 28, 2011

Dear Costco, and [*three names redacted*]:

It is the custom of our club members to report on matters such as these, both in prose and "poetry." We set out below our taste-test report in prose in respect to your hot dog. Our report in rhyme is a letter attachment to this e-mail.

At the outset all four members of our club wish to thank Costco for being flexible and open minded enough to listen to our complaint, to take it seriously, to take effective steps to find out what the problem was and then to fix it. We believe that when a business establishment exhibits that type of concern for the quality of its product and for its customers' interests, it will, surely succeed, as Costco obviously has.

We enjoyed meeting all three of you and thank you for the courtesies that Costco extended to us when we taste-tested their new hot dogs this Tuesday. We found that the hot dogs that we tasted on Tuesday were a definite improvement over the ones we complained about. We unanimously agreed that they were no longer soggy and therefore substantially improved in this regard. They had better color and the taste of the hot dog was not distorted by excessive moisture. Three of the four of us did not think that the hot dog was too garlicky and we thought they did taste good

Our fourth member did think his hot dog was too garlicky. Aside from that complaint, (which as one of you commented may be a function of personal circumstances including individual tastes, etc.), none of us had any other complaints about the hot dogs and feel that they were much improved over the ones we complained about.

So thank you for the courtesies extended to us throughout in successfully resolving our complaint. We'll be back next Thursday.

Yours truly,

Lou the Guru, Frank Frankfurter, Willy the Great of Infinite Palate, and Poet Larry-Eh*

Enc:
Poem re: Report on our Taste Test

D. Report In Poetry of Taste-Test

From The Gents of Former Laments

Dear Costco;

It was but a day or two ago
That the four Gourmet Gents
Of former hot dog laments
Were delighted
To be kindly invited
By Saul, Kevin and Antonio*
To Woodbine go,
To test-taste the Costco
Newly processed hot dog.

As we're not bumps on a log.
We made great haste
As men of good taste,
To enjoy another of our gourmet adventures,
And so we quickly inserted our dentures
Accepted your gracious invite
And attended at Woodbine for this Gourmet delight.

There we met the three food Musketeers of Costco
Saul, Kevin and Antonio*
We, four gourmets, including
The self-indulging
Willy the Great, Lou the Guru,
Frank Frankfurter too
And me, poet Larry-Eh
Tested the hot dogs of 100% beef
And to our great and below stated relief

Frank Frankfurter, Lou the Guru,
And Poet Larry-eh,
Voted a positive yea.
And accepted,
That the dogs' problems were bested.

However, Willy the Great
Of famed palate,
Had tasted the garlic,
Not once, but twice.
There's too much spice!
Yet he ate
Every morsel on his plate.

Oh Costco Oh Costco,
We say without jest
That the result of our test
Is that your dogs are darn good
And we would
Unanimously have voted
That you had 100 % done the trick
But for Willy's excessive sensitivity to garlic.

Our thanks to Costco,
Saul, Kevin and Antonio*
For successfully fixing
And not out of hand nixing
The serious and sincere laments
Of these four elderly gents.

Thanks Costco for addressing our hot dog concerns. That was great!
Something other corporations could learn from and ought to imitate

Oh Costco! Oh Costco!
Everyone knows

How your hot dog goes
So goes Costco
Oh Costco! Oh Costco!

Yours sincerely,
Frank Frankfurter, Lou the Guru
Poet Larry-Eh And Willy the Great, too.*

*Except for my name, all other names were changed or altered to protect privacy issues.

-90-

I get all kinds of spurious e-mails dealing with the ridiculous and sublime, and my experience in that regard is chronicled in a short article mixing biblical and scientific history.

The Computer And The Internet:
Their Story In The Context Of Biblical History

Here is the e-mail I just received from the Garden of Eden's Serpent. He is the official biographer for Adam and Eve. It purports to revise history a little by highlighting recently released allegations involving a biblical version of the history of the computer and the internet.

"Dear Larry,

Re: Dorothy*Com*, (popularly known as Dot Com), Co- Inventor Of The Biblical Computer and The Internet:

The original manner of messaging in the Garden of Eden was by a mobile drum. The earliest drum used was invented by Eve. She called it the kettledrum. Dot, (Eve's Garden of Eden undisclosed and illegitimate child), when young, banged on the kettledrum day and night without stop. The noise got so bad that the family was taken to the *Beth Din*. This is the Jewish Court, presided over by the Lord Chief

Justice in the Garden of Eden. The Lord heard the case and issued an injunction against Dot Com and her family. They were ordered to cease and desist *hucking a chainick* after they were convicted of disturbing the peace.

It was after this verdict that I, the Garden of Eden Serpent, introduced Eve to the apple of the tree of knowledge. She stupidly stole an apple from it, took a *byte* or two, and gave it to Adam who did the same. The apple was a *Macintosh*.

This apple was found in the couple's possession with a large chunk missing. They were charged and were convicted of *keeping a piece* and, as they were second offenders, they and their offspring were evicted from the Garden of Eden, and branded with a bitten apple tattooed on their foreheads as a symbol of their shame.

With their ill-gotten knowledge, they and their kin became very astute and invented an Apple computer. After that invention, Moses went to great heights to obtain operating instructions for their computer and managed to get to see the Pearly Gates and met with the *Surly Gates*.

Then after descending from Mount Sinai, Moses presented the Israelites with two tablets containing 10 effective operating instructions. These were later refined by the 613 Talmudic rules.

These tablets were very heavy as they were made of huge stones and contained very large print. Help was needed to make these heavy tablets portable. *Surly Gates* was called and he came to the rescue to solve the problem and he did. He replaced the stone with soft, light plastics and some metal stripping, and made the printing very small. In addition, Gates in honour of Moses, described the new word program as the Moses Speciality program now known as *MS WORD*. His lighter, stone-less tablets are now known as Micro*soft* computers.

Rapid growth and riches followed. However, such were not caused by the wise prophets, but rather by huge profits. Gates' major competitor was Job. He had experienced the Lord's wrath for his meddling in Gates' work. Job did his penance as described in the Book of Job, and thereafter saw the light. Job then went from rags to riches, and from a self-effacing, humble, God-fearing, human, to one of the world's most egotistical men, who started everything that he invented with the letter 'i.'

Mankind and his computer have suffered as well. They have experienced some current biblical plagues of yore, which in modern times include to name but a few:

'Bugs,' instead of grass hoppers, 'blue crash screens' instead of blood red rivers, and viruses instead of sickness and pestilence.

You will no doubt note that up to, and in recent times, women have not received any credit for Dot Com's brilliant work regarding the internet. So personally, to correct that historical error, I do, in the biblical sense, bless her as a women and say, 'Ah...men.'

Yours truly,
The Serpent"

Glossary:
Beth Din: Yiddish and means Court.
Hucking a chainick: Yiddish and literally means banging a teakettle. Figuratively it includes bothering someone by making too much noise.

-91-

A former colleague asked me for my views on a Supreme Court of the United States' judgement he sent to me in an article. I replied by e-mail.

An Ethical Lawyer?

Thank you for the article describing the U.S. Supreme Court's decision and its finding that the American Constitution does not provide American citizens with a right to an ethical lawyer when involved in litigation.

It is my view that this conclusion is not founded so much on legal precedent but on historical and practical concerns first learned from the French, (specifically from Napoleon) who, when preparing to marry his Josephine, ordered that the bridal consultant of the time seek out 50 Parisian virgins to be Josephine's bride's maids. That project was abandoned by Napoleon when not even one such virgin could be found in all of Paris.

The U.S. Supreme Court, in my view and reading between the lines of the decision, took guidance from the Napoleon situation and concluded that no one has **ever** established the existence of an ethical lawyer in all of the U.S.A., and therefore The Founding Fathers of the United States could not have stipulated in the Constitution for a right to one.

The decision is perfectly logical. However, it is interesting to note that in these two situations, neither the shortages experienced by Josephine at her time of need, nor by the current litigant when he needed an ethical lawyer, precluded either of them from being royally screwed.

INDEX

	Poem Name	Page Number
1.	Poetry Is Fun Isn't It?	8
2.	Neither Justice Nor Law	9
3.	Inward, Outward And Downward Bound	10
4.	Languishing At Home Alone	11
5.	The View From My 75th Birthday	12
6.	China	13
7.	Not Old, Just Aging	14
8.	What, Me Worry?	15
9.	The Hipster	16
10.	The Lexophile	17
11.	The Rose	18
12.	My One and Only	19
13.	The Colonoscopy	19
14.	Hair	21
15.	Global Warming?	22
16.	Don't Pooh Pooh Our Canada Goose	23
17.	The Hot Dog	23
18.	Has Been Or Never Was?	24
19.	A Journey To The Sun	25
20.	Chicken Wings	26

21.	The Old Apple Tree Of Despair	27
22.	The Adverb	28
23.	The Music Of Love	30
24.	Alzheimer's Man	31
25.	Expropriation Without Compensation	32
26.	Ignorance Is Not Bliss	33
27.	Greed	34
28.	The Shingles Patient	35
29.	Come Walk With Me	36
30.	The Coming Of Age	37
31.	Genius And Common Sense	38
32.	The Give And Take of Greed	39
33.	The Original Abolitionists	40
34.	My Advice To You Today	43
35.	Mindless	43
36.	Oh Yes I Can! (Israel's Toilet Boutique)	44
37.	I Am A Person	45
38.	Puff Puff: The Magic Drag-on	47
39.	The Golfer	48
40.	Goodbye, Toronto Gravy Train	49
41.	The Gas Line	50
42.	The Love Poem	51

43.	Mah Jongg	52
44.	Erosion	53
45.	Leave With A Smile	54
46.	An El Salvador Wedding	54
47.	Canadians Come to Florida	55
48.	Autumn's Sign	56
49.	An Imaginative Gadget	57
50.	A Loss Due To A Gain	58
51.	Barbados Bound	59
52.	The Ocean-Going Cruise	60
53.	A Non-Believer's Day At The Synagogue	61
54.	An Anti-Establishment Mess	62
55.	A Swelling Of The Head	63
56.	Ms. Sheila Regrets She's Unable To Attend	64
57.	Justice In Traffic Court	65
58.	Neither Here, Nor There—Neither Hen, Nor Hare	65
59.	English Bob, Or Kabob	66
60.	In Praise Of The Measure Of Man	67
61.	The Chinese Silver Pocket Full	67
62.	My Lighthouse	68
63.	Complement, Or Compliment	69
64.	What A Nice Old Man	70

65.	Toronto, The Pan Am Gamester	70
66.	Of Smoke And Mirrors	71
67.	Canadian Ground Hogs	72
68.	An Unforgettable Get Together	73
69.	Why Penguins Don't Fly	75
70.	Unchanging	75
71.	Trees	76
72.	Birthday Greetings To A Friend	78
73.	Two Careers	80
74.	My Beautiful Sister	81
75.	There's no Billable Time For Poetry	83
76.	Ugh! A Hot Dog With Beans	84
77.	Not a Trifling Matter	84
78.	Kindred Souls	85
79.	Pegasus ll	86
80.	Friendship	87
81.	Philomena	88
82	Retirement	90
83.	The Love of a Daughter And Mother	91
84.	So What If I Can't Spell	93
85.	When Can Cows Give Milk?	93
86.	Is Silence Golden?	94

87.	The Firefly	94
88.	Hope and Pray	95

Articles

89	Oh Costco! Oh Costco!	96
90.	The Computer and the Internet	104
91.	An Ethical Lawyer?	106

ABOUT THE AUTHOR

I was born in the City of Toronto in 1937 where I have resided continuously for 78 years. I have been married for 56 years to the love of my life, Sheila. We have three children, and they have blessed us with 6 grandchildren.

During my school years in Toronto, I earned an arts degree in a philosophy major at the University of Toronto, followed by a law degree at Osgoode Hall. I began a litigation practice in 1963.

Approximately 12 years later, I was made a Queens Counsel. I practiced law in the Courts initially as a trial lawyer and latterly as a Member of The Immigration and Refugee Board of Canada in the Immigration Appeal Division of that Board. I retired after 11 years on the Board at age 72.

As a lawyer and judicial officer my writing for over 40 years consisted mostly of Court briefs and judgements. Upon retirement, and during the last 6 years, I cast aside technical writing and engaged in what I call *pop poetry*...namely unstructured, humorous and serious rhyme about anything and everything.

[FIN]

www.ingramcontent.com/pod-product-compliance
Lightning Source LLC
Chambersburg PA
CBHW061334040426
42444CB00011B/2908